The Passive Income Dream

Jane Keeley et al.

Published by Jane Keeley, 2024.

THE PASSIVE INCOME DREAM

First edition. June 16, 2024.

ISBN: 979-8227657916

Written by Jane Keeley et al..

Foreword

A mobile hairstylist visited my home a few weeks ago. We were making small talk, as you do when you get your hair done.

The young woman explained that she had a young son and had found it difficult to sustain her full-time salon job since his arrival.

She had given up her position in favour of self-employment as a mobile stylist to help her achieve a better work-life balance.

I told her that I had done the same when my child was small and that now I work at home and mostly live off a passive income.

The hairstylist looked both surprised and impressed and said that a home-based passive income was her dream. She had tried some affiliate marketing on social media and made five pounds.

I pointed out that she had set up an affiliate account somewhere and had proven that she could make money this way. So why didn't she continue and aim to scale this into enough money that she could stay at home?

As with most people, her reply was simply that she hadn't got around to it. Life had gotten in the way.

It was different for me. I had the dream, worked out a plan, and executed it. I stayed awake and worked at it late at night, and in all of the moments when I felt inspired.

I don't (yet) make a fortune, however, I work at home, choose my hours, have enough to live on, and I make money while I am asleep.

The hairstylist suggested that I teach people how to make a passive income.

And so I have written this book.

I am not claiming to be a mega guru or anything. Neither am I fake, talking the talk and not walking the walk. I really do make a passive income. It currently sits at around £1,200 a month and I am hoping to double it within a year.

Passive income is in most cases not a get rich quick scheme.

Neither is it actually passive. You have to work at it. Thinking or dreaming about it won't earn you a penny. You need to create content or digital products, invest money, find something that works for you, and repeat, repeat, repeat.

I have heard so many people say, I would love to write a book, I would like to make money from my photography, it would be awesome to have a blog that generates some money. And so on.

But people all too often don't ever do these things. It just remains a dream.

Only by action will you reap rewards.

My dream of a large passive income will remain ongoing as long as I am able to work. I add to my portfolio of income streams daily. If I feel tired and need a break I might only work one or two days in a week.

This is the joy of being your own boss and in control of your finances. You create for yourself a lifestyle of time freedom and when you are exhausted or crisis hits, you can take a step back for a while.

There are multiple ways of earning a passive income. This book covers many of them. I may have missed out some methods, purely through lack of knowledge (as I already said, not an omnipotent guru).

Furthermore, the information in the book concentrates on the ways that I make a passive income, because that is what I know the most about.

At the back of the book, you will find signposting to further resources on the topic of passive income. You can then do some research and most importantly, start working to turn your dream into reality.

Thank you for reading, I appreciate it very much.

Disclaimer

<hr>

This book is about my personal experiences with my dream of building up a passive income to sustain myself and my small family.

I have been working towards my financial goals for years, and it is an ongoing endeavour.

I am not a financial expert or advisor, and there is no guarantee that following the information in this book will lead to financial success.

Any investment of time or money made as a result of reading this book is taken at your own risk. You can lose money as well as make it.

Always consult a qualified and experienced financial advisor before making any capital investment.

Make sure you follow local laws regarding reporting of income when you set out to make a passive income.

Work after birth

———

When a child suddenly enters your life, whether through birth, adoption, or other means, nothing is ever the same.

I had my first baby at the age of 27. I was married and we were lucky enough that I was able to stay at home for three years without earning any money.

Even more fortunately, I had the opportunity to study for a degree once my daughter hit the milestones of nursery and then school age.

This all occurred in the 1990s and 2000s when money seemed to go a little further than it does now. Childcare was a tad more affordable and investing in education was something that I felt could only be beneficial to the future of my family and daughter.

After several years of study, and many hours of juggling related stress and tears, I acquired a first-class honours degree and a professional qualification in social work.

This is when real stress began to take over my life. I started to work full-time, and in the field of social work, as with many other professional roles, this was certainly no 9 to 5. It was at least a 60 hour working week and I often didn't get home until after 9pm

I was young enough to cope with the energy required for the work. However, I felt like I hardly ever saw my daughter.

She would be dropped off at the breakfast club and then collected by the after-school team. She would wait until either I or her father (we had a rota, as he was also working long hours) came to collect her each night at around 6 pm.

By the time we had all eaten and my daughter had been bathed etc, it was bedtime. Weekends were spent recovering from the week's work and catching up on housework.

It all took a massive toll on the relationship between me and my now ex-husband. We sadly split up, and looking back, the ensuing shared custody was almost a relief. I now had some days off where I could just work without having to juggle issues such as childcare and school runs.

Reading this now, it sounds horrendous. If I could go back in time, I would have simply left my job. I think I must have felt that after several years of study, the only logical thing to do was to use the resulting qualifications.

I continued to work and the salary was enough to sustain myself as a part-time single parent. I had no debts, there was food on the table, and I mostly enjoyed my job.

Indeed, apart from a 2-3 year break after the birth of my daughter, I had always been in full-time employment. I didn't know any different. It was what my parents had done, and I had done well at school. I had always found work that was sufficient to sustain myself pretty well.

I just got on with working full time, even though it was killing me emotionally. That is all I knew to do.

Now let us fast forward to my life when I turned 40.

In my late thirties, I was still working full-time as a social worker. My ex-husband remarried pretty much as soon as our divorce was finalised. The new wife had a daughter of her own and my child sort of became more theirs than mine. They had more money than me and there were fancy holidays, acting lessons, and wonderful day trips.

I do not want to dwell on this topic. It was painful at times. My daughter is now an adult and we are extremely close. She is happy and well-adjusted and so the fact that I took a backseat role as she was growing up didn't harm her. I think it was only me who struggled with it all.

The truth is, I was so busy working in a very demanding, stressful job that I wouldn't have been able to provide as good a family life as my ex and his new wife were offering. Or that is what I thought anyway. I used my child-free time at weekends to go out trying to build a new family by finding a partner.

But I remained single and at the age of 40, I became pregnant.

I was not in a settled relationship at this time and you may judge if you really must. I have been through all of that condemnation already and know what some people think.

The reason I have told you this somewhat sorry backstory is to get to the climax, the turning point, the revelation that I had about working and earning money if you like.

I was not going to put my second child through life with a mother who couldn't cope with life, because she was completely overwhelmed with her job.

And actually, the universe stepped in and took my hand, leading me out of the workplace, just as I was indeed starting to spiral down into a pit of despair.

Working for the local authority, I was fortunate enough to receive a generous maternity package. I stayed at home for about a year (the details are somewhat foggy now, this was 15 years ago).

To keep the maternity pay given in the period of absence it was necessary to go back to work for 6 months. I was in no position to pay even a small amount back so I found a nursery for my baby daughter and climbed back onto the full-time work treadmill.

It was horrible. I missed my baby so much and would often sit at my desk weeping. I remember at least one work colleague being irritated and telling me that I had to stop crying because I was making everyone else miserable. Get a grip and so on. I tried to.

The exhaustion took its toll, though. I could not tolerate the meanness and lack of understanding from some of my colleagues and in particular my supervisor. I remember being told off for something that I had done to the best of my ability but it was badly, awfully wrong. All I wanted to do was be at home with my child.

And yes, I chose to have her, I made my bed and I was lying in it. And it was very uncomfortable.

Anyway, after a couple of paychecks, I realised that actually, I was heading for a life of near poverty. This is due to the obscenely high cost of childcare, a worldwide phenomenon I think, unless you live somewhere sensible such as Sweden. Maybe even there, I am not certain.

I would have been much better off working fewer hours, for example, half a week or maybe three days. I knew that part-time work would have fit in much better with my family situation too. I would have been able to go out to toddler groups, for example. I was also of the opinion that being at home more would benefit my daughter. I could not bear the thought of another decade of breakfast, evening, and holiday clubs.

Now, in the UK you have the right to apply for your job to be changed to part-time. Your company is obligated to consider your offer and get back to you with a timely decision. This was at least the case when I put in my application.

I was immediately told no. The reason given is that working part-time would not suit the needs of the business. This is a legitimate and legal reason for a company to decline a part-time working request.

I was quite upset. However, I did not take the decision personally as a few other women had recently had babies and they were all knocked back for part-time work too.

I paired up with one of them and we put forward a job share proposal. Together we would be the two halves of a full-time member of staff and share the workload as if we were one person.

Our request was declined, of course. The senior manager took me to one side and told me that I had to choose between being a social worker and being a mother. Bearing in mind that my job was supporting families and children, I was rather taken aback. I was a mother and here was the (female) boss telling me I could not therefore be a social worker.

I, and all of the other women who weren't being allowed to work part-time, left as soon as the 6 months were up. It felt like a purge but there was nothing we could do. The choice was full-time or nothing.

I cancelled the nursery and took my little treasure home from there one last time, full of relief, joy and a little trepidation.

And you know what, I have never looked back.

I took a little break (I had some savings) and then I gathered myself together and registered myself as self-employed.

Fifteen years later, I am still single and living very happily with my amazingly kind, fantastic teenage daughter. I have not worked for anyone apart from myself in all this time, and I am financially better off than I have ever been.

Whilst I did not start my self-employment journey with a focus on making a passive income, that side of my work has turned out to be far more profitable than the other sources.

Whilst I do have an online shop where I sell physical products, I recently decided to no longer buy any more stock. I shall keep it open and just let everything sell out. I am going all in with building a larger passive income.

What is a passive income?

Let us look more closely at what the term passive income means.

Passive income refers to earnings derived from activities in which the individual is not actively involved on a day-to-day basis. Unlike active income, which typically involves continuous effort (like a salary from a job), passive income is generated with minimal ongoing effort once the initial work or investment is in place.

What are some examples of passive income?

Rental Income: Money earned from renting out property, such as apartments, houses, or commercial spaces.

Dividends: Earnings from owning shares in a company, where the company pays out a portion of its profits to shareholders.

Interest Income: Income from interest-bearing accounts, bonds, or other financial instruments.

Royalties: Payments received from intellectual property like books, music, patents, or trademarks.

Capital Gains: Profits from the sale of investments, such as stocks, real estate, or other assets.

Business Income: Profits from businesses in which the owner is not actively involved in day-to-day operations, often through ownership of a limited partnership or shares in a corporation.

<u>Online Content Revenue</u> from online activities like blogging, vlogging, or digital products (e.g., eBooks, courses), where content generates income over time.

Online content revenue is how I have chosen to make my passive income, and most of this book will focus on this arena.

The key aspect of passive income is that after the initial setup or investment, the income stream requires little to no effort to maintain. This type of income is often sought by people seeking financial independence and wealth building.

A good way to look at passive income is to compare it to planting a fruitful garden. You may spend many, many hours planting your garden. Perhaps you invest a large amount of money in top-quality, expensive soil which will make your plants grow faster and higher. Maybe you don't have much cash to invest so instead it is your time and talent that are the main factors causing your garden to flourish.

Over time, and at varying speeds dependent on hours worked and level of financial investment, your garden will mature and you will be able to earn from what you have planted and nurtured.

What is so enticing about the idea of earning a passive income?

The idea of a passive income stream is enticing for several reasons:

<u>Financial Freedom</u>: Passive income can provide a steady revenue stream that is not tied to the amount of time or effort put in. This allows individuals to achieve financial independence and reduce reliance on traditional employment.

<u>Flexibility and Time</u>: With passive income, people can have more control over their time. They can pursue other interests, hobbies, or entrepreneurial ventures without being constrained by a 9 to 5 job.

<u>Diversification of Income</u>: Relying solely on a single source of income can be risky. Passive income allows for diversification, reducing the financial impact if one income stream fails.

<u>Wealth Building</u>: Passive income streams, especially those that involve investments like real estate or stocks, can contribute to long-term wealth accumulation. The compounding effect of reinvesting earnings can significantly enhance financial growth over time.

<u>Security</u>: Having multiple income streams can provide a financial safety net in case of job loss, economic downturns, or unexpected expenses. This security can reduce stress and improve overall quality of life.

<u>Scalability</u>: Many passive income opportunities, such as digital products or investments, can be scaled without a proportional increase in effort. This scalability can lead to substantial income growth.

<u>Retirement Planning</u>: Passive income is often a key component of retirement planning. It can supplement retirement savings and provide a continuous income stream during retirement, helping to maintain a desired lifestyle.

<u>Legacy and Generational Wealth</u>: Passive income streams, especially those involving investments and real estate, can be passed down to future generations, helping to create generational wealth.

The allure of passive income lies in the potential to achieve greater financial stability, freedom, and the ability to pursue a more balanced and fulfilling life.

My discovery of the existence of passive income streams was accidental. I started my self-employment with an eBay store. Having a young child at that time, I was aware of what people in a similar situation wanted to buy for their growing families.

I researched what sort of baby-related products were selling well on eBay, and applied to several wholesale suppliers so that I could purchase stock.

I didn't have massive amounts of cash to invest, but I wasn't looking to make huge amounts of money. I guess you could call what I was aiming for a lifestyle business, a way to make enough money to be able to afford life by working at home.

Leopard print baby socks were my best seller, closely followed by some cute little headbands and hats for new babies. Now, I am rather crafty and I began to make little headbands instead of buying them wholesale. The raw materials were very cheap and they began to return a decent profit.

I am also able to knit, and I discovered the world of newborn photography props. I was able to quite quickly whip up some unusual, very cute, newborn knitted hats and they were eagerly bought by photographers. In those days, big, chunky baby hats with huge pom poms and elf tails were very popular. Newborn photography was relatively new and I kept my prices low to attract newcomers to this artistic field.

Of course, none of what I have just described is at all passive. It was incredibly hard work. And the profit was low. I had to buy stock and materials, make the products, list them for sale, market them, deal with buyers, wrap parcels, and walk or bus ride to the post office daily.

As well as having an eBay store, I started to sell my handmade goods on Etsy. It is there that I noticed a surge in independent designers creating and selling their patterns in digital format. Using knitting as an example, you can design something very simple, such as a hat, and carefully write out the instructions so that other people can make your designs.

On Etsy, you can upload this piece of work as a digital file and customers will order it (if it is good enough to attract buyers of course) and they then receive a downloaded electronic copy.

I remember writing in a Facebook group that it must be cool to make money this way because you just design the pattern and then collect the money. I was, quite rightly, shot down in flames by several knitters. They told me that designing knitting patterns takes many hours and a great deal of talent and that it is not easy money but extremely hard work

I wanted to try it, though. I had designed a hat for my older daughter, a funky piece that was very unusual to look at, and yet very easy to knit. I wrote down how to knit it and knit a few more from my instructions. I knew the pattern was perfect, and I took some photos of my daughter modelling it. I listed it for sale in my Etsy store and waited.

To cut a long story short, this digital item (a downloadable PDF file) is still for sale now and I have sold hundreds of copies of this knitting pattern. I have added several more knitting patterns to my Etsy store, and have now also written a few knitting pattern books which I self-published on Amazon. As the years have flown by, I have opened a total of 4 Etsy stores and sell several different types of digital files. Variations of products include templates, art papers, clip art, and journals.

I make a passive income from these digital files which is enough to live on, and I am still building my portfolio. I am not rich, and this was never my intention. What I have achieved was exactly what I asked from the universe - enough money to live on whilst staying at home and looking after my daughter.

It hasn't been easy and I really must stress that a passive income is not 'doing nothing'. More and more people are chasing the passive income dream. The competition is fierce, and of course, with a cost of living crisis, people do not have as much spare income to buy all of the digital products that they may like.

I have only personally tapped into a tiny particle of the passive income market. In this book, we will look more closely at the field of selling digital products on Etsy, as well as other avenues of passive income. I have tried some of the methods of making passive cash within these pages, but not all.

I hope that I can help you gain a realistic look at what it takes to build a passive stream and assist with your decision about where, and indeed whether at all, to invest your time and money to start a passive income journey.

Selling digital products

Selling digital products to make a passive income is a large field. As you already know, I sell several different types of files on Etsy. I chose Etsy because I was familiar with this platform, and mostly it works ok.

I do, however, spend a considerable time each day answering emails because for some reason many customers do not receive their downloaded files. This is annoying both for me, and them, and I still have no understanding about why the seemingly simple download system does not always work.

In addition to this, the seller fees on Etsy have massively increased since I first went into business. Honestly, I seem to only receive half of the profit that I once did. Etsy is a company that went public in 2015. The platform is now full of non-handmade goods posing as handmade and getting found in the huge swamp of digital products for sale can be difficult.

Having said all of this, the footfall of shoppers on Etsy is huge, and the company does invest heavily in advertising. I do no marketing of my products. This is because I am just one person and there isn't enough time to do everything that I should be doing to promote my business. I am happy with the sales obtained from Etsy, and therefore I continue despite the fees that they take before I see any profit.

Please take a look at the Etsy platform. Digital files are marked on item listings so that people (should) know they are buying a download and not a physical item. You will find a huge variety of digital products for sale. Photographs, posters, background images, mock-ups, templates, journals, patterns, clip art, illustrations, posters, templates, and items that people print out themselves or use as elements for their digital work.

I recently purchased a little cutting machine. It does things like cutting out images from heat transfer vinyl, and you then iron the cutout onto t-shirts or perhaps bags. The files needed are called SVG files, and I have noticed a recent surge of this type of digital file for sale on Etsy. Indeed, I bought a package of SVG cat files from Etsy so that I could create some fun cat shopping bags to give to friends and family.

If you are interested in selling digital files on Etsy, you need to pick something that you feel confident in creating. Open a shop, and preferably open an Instagram and Pinterest account in the same name. Find your market, upload your files, and wait for the magic to happen. It does take time, and the more items in your store, and the more marketing you do, the easier and faster you will be found and the more money you will make.

Etsy is not the only platform available for selling digital files.

Once you have created some digital files to sell, you need not only list them on Etsy. You can indeed start your own website. Platforms such as Shopify, for example, allow for the selling of downloadable digital files.

I have avoided selling on my own website. This is because of an EU law around the sales of digital products. If you sell an instant download (not applicable if you manually email files yourself) to a customer in the EU, you are required to collect the VAT on each product and pay it to the country of the buyer's residence.

Imagine you sell hundreds of files per week and several customers are based in every country within the EU. What a headache for a small trader. I can feel my temples causing my brain to burst even thinking about the mechanics of working out how to pay the required VAT.

I envisage a huge cloud of fines and bills for incorrect VAT payment landing on my head, most of them from Germany, a country that loves to make people pay for indiscretions of their beloved EU laws (yes, they got me once - I missed out a legally required sentence when trying to sell a hat online in their country and copped a large fine).

Anyway, I think the law was to gain correct VAT payments for the big boys such as Amazon. If you sell on a platform such as Etsy, who process all of the financial payments themselves, it is then their responsibility to collect and pay the VAT. I have not been brave enough to deviate from this platform. I have set it up, the listings are there. I write down every payment I receive from them and send the figures to the tax man, and all I have to do is work at making more digital products and dealing with emails as mentioned before.

There are several other platforms available for selling digital products. I have carried out some research and have tried to provide a comprehensive list below. Please check them out to see whether your products may fit their service. Some of the platforms require an application and they will decide whether or not you can sell with them.

What are some popular platforms where you can sell digital files?

Etsy: Known for handmade and vintage items, Etsy also has a thriving marketplace for digital downloads such as printable art, planners, and digital invitations.

Gumroad: A platform that allows creators to sell digital products directly to their audience. It's suitable for eBooks, software, music, and other digital goods.

Sellfy: An easy-to-use platform for selling digital products, physical goods, and subscriptions. It also provides tools for marketing and sales analytics.

Shopify: A comprehensive e-commerce platform that supports the sale of digital products through various apps and plugins.

Amazon Kindle Direct Publishing (KDP): Ideal for authors, KDP allows you to self-publish eBooks and paperbacks for sale on Amazon.

Creative Market: A marketplace for design assets such as graphics, fonts, templates, and other digital design resources.

Envato Market: Includes sites like ThemeForest (themes and templates), AudioJungle (music and sound effects), VideoHive (stock videos and motion graphics), and GraphicRiver (graphics and vectors).

Teachable: Primarily for online courses, Teachable also supports the sale of digital products like eBooks and downloadable content as part of course packages.

Payhip: A simple platform for selling digital downloads and memberships directly from your website or through Payhip's store.

Blurb: Allows you to create, publish, and sell high-quality photo books, trade books, magazines, and eBooks.

BigCommerce: An e-commerce platform that supports the sale of digital products with various customization options.

E-junkie: A service for selling digital downloads and tangible goods with secure delivery and extensive integration options.

Patreon: While primarily a subscription platform, Patreon allows creators to offer digital downloads as rewards to their patrons.

Thinkific: An online course platform that also allows you to sell digital products like eBooks and other downloadable resources.

<u>Squarespace</u>: Offers e-commerce functionality to sell digital products directly from your website built on Squarespace.

<u>Redbubble</u>: While primarily for print-on-demand products, Redbubble also supports selling digital designs that customers can download.

<u>Selfy</u>: A versatile platform that offers tools for selling both physical and digital products, with a focus on creatives and small businesses.

These platforms cater to different types of digital products, so you can choose one that best fits the nature of your digital files and your target audience.

Don't forget to find out whether or not you will be required to collect any necessary VAT or additional taxes. If so, and your business is large enough, I recommend using an accountant to help make sure you are meeting all legal and financial requirements.

A quick note about self-employment

⸺

If you are making a passive income, you are in business.

You may therefore need to register yourself as self-employed.

How much you can earn before needing to register will depend on where you live.

In the UK I keep reading that you can make a thousand pounds before having to register. I am not sure whether or not this is accurate.

I strongly recommend consulting your responsible tax office before you go into the business of making a passive income stream, and at least when you start to make some money.

You can be self-employed alongside a regular job so don't worry, and until you are making a massive income your tax payments probably won't be affected.

If you strike it lucky and begin to make a very good income, I would recommend seeking financial advice from an accountant or similar.

Your time and energy should be going into growing your passive income, and not dealing with the headache of filling in tax forms.

Amazon Kindle Direct Publishing (KDP)

———

One of my passive income streams comes from self-publishing books via Amazon Kindle Direct Publishing (KDP).

Indeed, this book that you are reading is one such product.

I have written and self-published several books and would like to use this experience to talk about this platform further.

Here is an overview of Amazon KDP:

Amazon Kindle Direct Publishing (KDP) is a self-publishing platform that allows authors to publish and distribute their books directly to Amazon's global marketplace. It offers a straightforward way for writers to reach a wide audience without the need for a traditional publishing contract.

Here are some key features and benefits of Amazon KDP:

What are the key features of Amazon KDP?

<u>Ease of Use</u>: KDP is user-friendly, allowing authors to upload their manuscripts and cover designs in various formats, such as Word or PDF.

<u>Global Reach</u>: Books published through KDP are available on Amazon's international websites, providing access to millions of potential readers worldwide.

<u>Royalty Options</u>: Authors can choose between two royalty options, 35%, and 70%, depending on the book's price and distribution settings.

<u>Print-On-Demand</u>: KDP also offers print-on-demand services for paperback books, meaning books are printed only when ordered, reducing the need for inventory and upfront costs.

<u>Marketing Tools</u>: KDP provides various promotional tools, such as Kindle Countdown Deals and Free Book Promotions, to help authors market their books.

<u>Real-Time Sales Tracking</u>: Authors can track their sales and royalties in real-time through their KDP dashboard.

<u>KDP Select</u>: Enrolling in KDP Select gives authors access to additional promotional tools and allows their books to be part of Kindle Unlimited and the Kindle Owners' Lending Library, potentially increasing exposure and earnings.

Benefits of Amazon KDP

<u>Control and Flexibility</u>: Authors retain control over their work, including pricing, rights, and the ability to make updates or corrections at any time.

<u>Cost-Effective</u>: There are no upfront costs to publish through KDP. Amazon takes a percentage of the sales as a fee. Amazon does take a large percentage, however, you set your prices.

<u>Quick Publishing Process</u>: Once a book is uploaded and submitted, it can be available for sale on Amazon within 24 to 72 hours.

<u>Great Revenue Potential</u>: With higher royalty rates than many traditional publishing deals, KDP can be financially rewarding, especially for popular or niche books.

<u>Excellent Support and Resources</u>: Amazon provides a wealth of resources, including detailed guides and a support team, to help authors navigate the publishing process.

How does selling books on Amazon KDP work?

The following steps will help you to start self-publishing on Amazon:

1. <u>Create an Account</u>: Sign up for a KDP account using your existing Amazon account or create a new one.
2. <u>Prepare Your Manuscript</u>: Format your manuscript according to KDP guidelines and create a cover design. Amazon has a cover creation tool that you can use if you decide not to make your own book cover.
3. <u>Upload Your Book</u>: Upload your manuscript and cover file to the KDP platform.
4. <u>Set Your Pricing</u>: Choose your royalty plan and set the price for your book.
5. <u>Publish</u>: Submit your book for review and publication. Once approved, it will be available for purchase on Amazon.

Amazon KDP democratises the publishing process, enabling authors to publish their work easily and reach a global audience without the barriers typically associated with traditional publishing.

To self-publish a book on Amazon, you don't even need to write a book. You can produce what is called a low-content book.

A low-content book is a type of book that requires minimal writing and is primarily composed of repetitive content or blank pages designed for users to fill in.

These books typically include items such as journals, planners, notebooks, sketchbooks, colouring books, and logbooks. They are popular among self-publishers on Amazon KDP because they are relatively easy to create and can be produced quickly.

Characteristics of Low Content Books:

<u>Minimal Text</u>: They have little to no text content, focusing instead on blank or patterned pages for the user to fill in.

<u>Simple Layouts</u>: The interior design is often simple and repetitive, such as lined pages, grids, prompts, or templates.

<u>High Demand</u>: These books cater to a wide range of niches and interests, making them popular among buyers for personal use, gifts, or organisational purposes.

<u>Creative Covers</u>: The cover design plays a crucial role in attracting buyers, often being more elaborate and visually appealing to stand out in the market.

Examples of Low Content Books:

<u>Journals and Diaries</u>: Blank or lined pages for writing.

<u>Planners and Organizers</u>: Pages with date formats, to-do lists, and goal-setting prompts.

<u>Notebooks</u>: Lined, dotted, or grid pages for notes, sketches, or bullet journaling.

<u>Logbooks</u>: Specific templates for tracking activities, such as fitness logs, expense trackers, or mileage logs.

<u>Colouring Books</u>: Pages with black-and-white illustrations for colouring.

<u>Sketchbooks</u>: Blank pages for drawing or sketching.

<u>Activity Books</u>: Simple puzzles, prompts, or activities, especially for children.

Why Publish Low Content Books on Amazon KDP?

<u>Ease of Creation</u>: These books are straightforward to design using basic tools like Microsoft Word, Adobe InDesign, or even online platforms like Canva.

<u>Quick Production</u>: Since they don't require extensive writing or editing, they can be produced and published quickly.

<u>Scalability</u>: Authors can produce multiple low-content books across various niches to maximise their market reach and potential revenue.

<u>Passive Income</u>: Once published, these books can generate a steady stream of passive income with little to no maintenance required.

<u>Customization</u>: Authors can easily create variations of a book (e.g., different covers, layouts, or themes) to appeal to different audiences.

How to go about creating a low-content book on Amazon KDP:

<u>Research</u>: Identify popular niches and types of low-content books that are in demand.

<u>Design the Interior</u>: Create the internal pages using design software, ensuring they are properly formatted according to KDP's guidelines.

<u>Design the Cover</u>: Create an eye-catching cover that will attract buyers. I always use Canva to design book covers.

<u>Format the Book</u>: Ensure the entire book (interior and cover) meets KDP's formatting requirements. Amazon KDP has all the information you need on their website - numerous excellent tutorials are aimed at beginners.

<u>Upload to KDP</u>: Upload the book to Amazon KDP, set your pricing, and choose your distribution channels.

<u>Publish and Promote</u>: Publish your book and use various marketing strategies to promote it.

Low-content books offer a unique opportunity for self-publishers to quickly and efficiently enter the market, capitalise on trending niches, and generate passive income.

I haven't personally ever produced or sold any low-content books. My best-selling books are collections of knitting patterns. I price my knitting pattern books low and have found that smaller collections at a low price sell the best. For example, my 6 cosy headband knitting patterns booklet costs only 99p for the Kindle version.

Selling 6 patterns for less than a pound brings great value to anyone looking to knit a headband. They can buy a paper copy as well as a Kindle e-book via the KDP print-on-demand service. This means that they don't have to read from a screen or print anything out. Paper copies of knitting patterns are useful because you can tick off each row as you knit it, for example.

Here is an overview of how to go about self-publishing both low-content and written books such as novels on the Amazon platform:

Starting to self-publish on Amazon KDP (Kindle Direct Publishing) is a straightforward process, but it requires careful planning and execution to ensure success. Here's a step-by-step guide to help you get started:

<u>Write Your Book</u>: Complete your manuscript, ensuring it is well-written and edited.

<u>Format the Manuscript</u>: Format your manuscript according to KDP's guidelines. Use tools like Microsoft Word, Scrivener, or Google Docs

for writing and formatting. Ensure the document is properly structured with appropriate headings, fonts, and spacing.

I personally write my books on Google docs and then format them using the Kindle Create app. I find this the easiest way to ensure that my books are properly constructed for publishing.

<u>Design the Cover</u>: Create a Professional Cover: Your book cover is crucial for attracting readers. You can design your cover using graphic design software like Adobe Photoshop or Canva, or hire a professional designer.

<u>Follow KDP Guidelines</u>: Ensure your cover meets KDP's size and resolution requirements.

<u>Set Up Your Amazon KDP Account</u>: Go to the Amazon KDP website and sign up using your existing Amazon account or create a new one. Complete your profile by filling in your author/publisher information, including payment and tax details.

<u>Upload your manuscript and cover</u>: Log into KDP, access your KDP dashboard, and select "Create a New Title." Enter the book details and provide all necessary information about your book, including title, author name, description, keywords, and categories. Upload your formatted manuscript and cover file. Ensure your files are correctly formatted to avoid any issues during the publishing process.

<u>Set your pricing and distribution</u>: Select the territories where you want your book to be available (e.g., worldwide). Decide on your book's price. Consider factors like length, genre, and competition. You can choose between two royalty plans (35% or 70%). You can then choose whether or not to enrol in KDP select. Enrolling in KDP Select gives you access to promotional tools and makes your book available on Kindle Unlimited and the Kindle Owners' Lending Library. You will

receive payments for page turns when people use the Kindle Unlimited facility and read your book for free.

Publish your book: Preview your book using KDP's online previewer to ensure everything looks correct. Once you are satisfied with the preview, click "Publish Your Kindle eBook" or "Publish Your Paperback" (if you're also publishing a print version).

Wait for Approval: Amazon will review your book, which can take up to 72 hours. Once approved, your book will be available for sale on Amazon.

Promote Your Book: It is a good idea to set up an Amazon Author Central page to connect with readers and manage your author profile.

Use social media platforms to announce your book launch and engage with potential readers. You can also consider running Amazon Advertising campaigns to increase your book's visibility. If enrolled in KDP Select, use promotional tools like Kindle Countdown Deals and Free Book Promotions to boost sales.

Track your sales: Use the KDP dashboard to monitor your sales and track your book's performance. Encourage readers to leave reviews and use this information to improve your future books. Make updates to your book's description, keywords, or even content based on reader feedback and sales performance.

Here are some more useful tips to help you get started with self-publishing:

Professional Editing: Consider hiring a professional editor to ensure your manuscript is polished.

Cover Design: Invest in a high-quality cover design; it's the first thing potential readers see.

<u>Continuous Learning</u>: Stay updated on KDP policies and best practices by reading the KDP Help section and participating in author forums and communities.

By following these steps, you can successfully self-publish your book on Amazon KDP and reach a global audience.

Amazon KDP is a great place to start your self-publishing journey. If you are a budding author, you may also be interested in other self-publishing platforms.

Here is a list of the most popular platforms for self-publishing books. I have included Amazon KDP as a comparison to the others:

<u>Amazon Kindle Direct Publishing (KDP)</u>

Features: Allows you to publish eBooks and paperbacks, offers global distribution, and provides promotional tools.

Best For: Authors looking for extensive reach and robust marketing tools.

<u>IngramSpark</u>

Features: Supports print and eBook publishing, offers wide distribution to bookstores and libraries, and high-quality print options.

Best For: Authors who want broad distribution beyond Amazon.

<u>Smashwords</u>

Features: Distributes eBooks to major retailers like Barnes & Noble, Apple Books, Kobo, and libraries.

Best For: Authors focusing on eBook distribution across multiple platforms.

Draft2Digital

Features: Easy-to-use platform for converting and distributing eBooks to multiple retailers, including Amazon, Apple Books, Barnes & Noble, and more.

Best For: Authors looking for a user-friendly, multi-platform eBook distributor.

Apple Books for Authors

Features: Direct access to publish eBooks on Apple Books, detailed analytics, and promotional tools.

Best For: Authors targeting Apple device users.

Kobo Writing Life

Features: Publish eBooks directly to Kobo's store, global distribution, and promotional opportunities through Kobo.

Best For: Authors focusing on international markets, especially in Canada, Europe, and Japan.

Barnes & Noble Press

Features: Self-publishing platform for eBooks and print books, available on the Barnes & Noble website.

Best For: Authors targeting the US market and Barnes & Noble's customer base.

Lulu

Features: Offers print-on-demand and eBook publishing, wide distribution options, and a variety of print formats.

Best For: Authors wanting to create high-quality print books and photo books.

Blurb

Features: Specialises in high-quality print books, including photo books, trade books, and magazines, with options for eBook publishing.

Best For: Authors focusing on visually rich books like photo books and art books.

Google Play Books

Features: Publish eBooks directly to Google's eBook store, with access to Google Play's global audience.

Best For: Authors seeking to reach Android users and leverage Google's vast ecosystem.

BookBaby

Features: Comprehensive self-publishing services including editing, design, printing, and distribution for both eBooks and print books.

Best For: Authors looking for a full-service self-publishing company.

StreetLib

Features: Global distribution for eBooks and print books, multiple language support, and royalty management.

Best For: Authors seeking international distribution and multi-language support.

Reedsy

Features: Marketplace for professional publishing services such as editing, design, and marketing, along with a book editor tool for formatting.

Best For: Authors looking for professional help with the publishing process.

PublishDrive

Features: Distribution to over 400 stores and 240,000 libraries, detailed sales analytics, and marketing tools.

Best For: Authors wanting extensive global reach and detailed performance insights.

These platforms offer various features and distribution options, allowing authors to choose the one that best fits their needs and goals. Whether you're focusing on eBooks, print books, or both, these platforms provide the tools and support necessary to successfully self-publish and distribute your work.

I have used Draft2Digital as well as Amazon KDP to self-publish my books. I find this company clunkier than Amazon when it comes to uploading my books. However, the profits are higher as they publish your work on multiple platforms, for example, Apple Books and Barnes & Noble, saving you the work of dealing with everyone on the above list. Draft2Digital also takes less of a cut than Amazon.

Draft2Digital can even publish to Amazon for you in certain circumstances, so you can just use them as a one-stop shop.

I use both Amazon and Draft2Digital, but in most cases just Amazon. This is because of the huge footfall on Amazon, and just the ease of the upload system. It makes my life easier and you can be paid for page turns (see previous information about KDP Select) if your work appears in digital format ONLY on the Amazon platform.

For further details about how to self-publish, please consult the websites of the platforms that you would like to sell with. This is the best place to get accurate and up-to-date information about how to start your self-publishing journey and the current fees and requirements etc.

The Amazon KDP website is particularly informative and contains tutorials as well as enlightening community posts from other users.

Content creation

My various streams of passive income fall under the umbrella of content creation.

The field of content creation is wide and varied. There is little financial start-up cost (assuming you already have a laptop or tablet/phone at your disposal), your main investment will be time and energy. Let us look further at the world of content creation. You can think about how you can utilise your specific talents and skills to make a passive income.

So what is content creation and does it make passive income?

Content creation involves producing material for various media, including text, images, video, and audio. This material can be educational, entertaining, informative, or promotional. The goal of content creation is often to engage an audience, drive traffic, and build a following. Here's how you can earn passive income from content creation:

Let us have a look at some of the types of content creation that can help you earn a passive income.

1. Blogging: Writing articles on specific topics of interest.

2. Vlogging: Creating video content, typically shared on platforms like YouTube.

3. Podcasting: Producing audio content, often in the form of episodic series.

4. Social Media Content: Posts, stories, and videos shared on platforms like Instagram, TikTok, and Facebook.

5. E-books and Digital Products: Writing and selling digital books, guides, or other downloadable products.

6. Online Courses: Creating educational content delivered through structured courses on platforms like Udemy or Teachable.

7. Photography and Graphic Design: Producing visual content that can be sold or licensed.

So what are some of the ways that you can use content creation to make a passive income?

<u>Advertising Revenue</u>

Blogging: Use platforms like Google AdSense to display ads on your blog. You earn money when visitors view or click on these ads.

YouTube: Join the YouTube Partner Program to earn money from ads displayed on your videos

<u>Sponsored Content</u>

Partner with brands to create content that promotes their products or services. Brands pay you for featuring their products in your content.

<u>Selling Digital Products</u>

Create and sell e-books, printables, stock photos, templates, or any other downloadable content. Once created, these products can be sold repeatedly without additional work.

<u>Online Courses and Membership Sites</u>

Develop courses or membership sites where users pay a fee to access your content. Platforms like Udemy, Teachable, and Patreon can help facilitate this.

<u>Royalties</u>

Earn royalties from content such as books, music, or designs. For example, self-published authors can earn royalties from book sales on Amazon KDP.

<u>Licensing</u>

Licence your content for use by others. This is common with photography, music, and software. We will look at stock photography in more detail soon.

<u>Subscription Models</u>

Offer premium content through a subscription model. Platforms like Substack for newsletters or OnlyFans for exclusive content can be utilised. Out of interest, OnlyFans is not only for nude pictures, but many people also post there with topics such as cooking or keeping fit.

<u>Affiliate Marketing</u>

Promote products or services through special affiliate links. You earn a commission for every sale made through your link. This can be done through blogs, videos, or social media posts.

To start in affiliate marketing, you need to sign up with one or more affiliate marketing companies. The Amazon Associates Program is a great place to start if you are a beginner. Here are some affiliate programmes that you may be interested in joining:

1. <u>Amazon Associates</u>

- One of the largest and most popular affiliate programs.

- Offers a wide range of products to promote.

- Commissions vary by product category.

2. <u>ShareASale</u>

- A well-established affiliate network with a large number of merchants.

- Offers a variety of products and services across different niches.

- User-friendly interface and robust reporting tools.

3. <u>CJ Affiliate (formerly Commission Junction)</u>

- One of the oldest and most reliable affiliate networks.

- Partners with many well-known brands.

- Comprehensive tools for tracking and reporting.

4. <u>Rakuten Advertising</u>

- Part of the Rakuten Group, a leading global e-commerce company.

- Offers a broad selection of merchants and products.

- Advanced tracking and reporting features.

5. <u>ClickBank</u>

- Specialises in digital products like eBooks, software, and online courses.

- High commission rates.

- Easy to join and start promoting products.

6. <u>Impact</u>

- Known for its advanced tracking and attribution tools.

- Works with a range of well-known brands.

- Focuses on performance marketing and partnerships.

7. <u>AWIN (Affiliate Window)</u>

- A global affiliate network with a wide range of advertisers.

- Offers extensive tools and resources for affiliates.

- Transparent reporting and payment systems.

8. <u>FlexOffers</u>

- A large affiliate network with a diverse range of advertisers.

- Offers real-time tracking and reporting.

- Competitive commission rates.

9. <u>AvantLink</u>

- Focuses on high-quality merchants and products.

- Advanced technology for tracking and analytics.

- Offers various tools for optimizing affiliate marketing efforts.

10. <u>Pepperjam</u>

- Provides a comprehensive affiliate marketing platform.

- Known for its advanced tracking and reporting capabilities.

- Works with a variety of top brands.

11. <u>PartnerStack</u>

- Designed for B2B SaaS affiliate programs.

- Focuses on driving partner and affiliate relationships.

- Robust tools for managing partnerships and tracking performance.

12. <u>eBay Partner Network</u>

- Allows affiliates to promote eBay listings.

- Commissions are based on the final sale price.

- Extensive tracking and reporting tools.

13. <u>MaxBounty</u>

- A performance-based affiliate network.

- Specialises in CPA (cost-per-action) offers.

- High payouts and a variety of offers to choose from.

14. <u>Refersion</u>

- Designed for e-commerce businesses.

- Integrates easily with platforms like Shopify, BigCommerce, and WooCommerce.

- Provides comprehensive tracking and reporting tools.

15. <u>Skimlinks</u>

- Automatically converts regular product links into affiliate links.

- Ideal for content publishers like bloggers and media websites.

- Partners with numerous merchants and advertisers.

Key Considerations When Choosing an Affiliate Marketing Platform:

1. Merchant Variety: Look for a platform that offers a wide range of merchants and products in your niche.
2. Commission Rates: Compare the commission rates and

payment terms.

3. Tracking and Reporting: Ensure the platform provides robust tracking and reporting tools to monitor your performance.
4. Support and Resources: Check for available support and resources to help you succeed as an affiliate.
5. Reputation: Consider the platform's reputation and reviews from other affiliates.

Summary so far

So far in the book, we have had a look at the two forms of content creation that make up the majority of my own passive income generation: selling digital files on Etsy and self-publishing books on Amazon KDP.

This income is made by actually selling digital products that you make yourself - the files and the books.

We have also learnt that it is possible to earn from your content via strategies such as advertising placement, affiliate marketing, and sponsorship.

If you are a total beginner to the field of earning a passive income via your content creation, it might seem overwhelming. Let us take a look at some steps you can follow to start earning from your content creation.

1. Identify Your Niche: Focus on a specific area where you have expertise or passion. This helps in attracting a dedicated audience.
2. Create High-Quality Content: Consistently produce valuable, engaging, and high-quality content. This builds trust and a loyal following.
3. Build an Audience: Use SEO (this is very important and we will delve into this area later), social media, and networking to grow your audience, engage with your followers, and build a community.
4. Monetize Your Content: Choose one or more monetization methods that suit your content type and audience (see

previous chapter).

5. Automate and Optimise: Use tools to automate tasks like social media posting and email marketing. Continuously optimise your content and strategies based on performance analytics.

6. Diversify Income Streams: Don't rely on just one source of income. Combine multiple monetization strategies to maximise your earnings.

By **consistently** creating valuable content and strategically monetizing it, you can build multiple streams of passive income. The initial effort in content creation can pay off over time as your audience grows and engages with your monetized content. A key factor here is consistency and again we will look at this topic in more depth further on in the book.

Here is a comprehensive list of platforms where you can earn passive income from your content creation. Your choice of where to start will depend on your chosen niche area and the type of content that you wish to create.

YouTube

How It Works: Earn money through ads, channel memberships, Super Chat, and YouTube Premium revenue.

Best For: Video creators and vloggers.

Medium

How It Works: Earn money based on member reading time through the Medium Partner Program.

Best For: Writers and bloggers.

Patreon

How It Works: Offer exclusive content to subscribers who pay a monthly fee.

Best For: Creators with a dedicated following in any content type (video, audio, writing, art).

<u>Substack</u>

How It Works: Publish newsletters and earn subscription fees from your readers.

Best For: Writers and journalists.

<u>Teachable</u>

How It Works: Create and sell online courses. Earn money whenever someone enrols in your course.

Best For: Educators and experts in specific fields.

<u>Udemy</u>

How It Works: Create and sell online courses. Udemy handles marketing and sales.

Best For: Educators and trainers.

<u>Skillshare</u>

How It Works: Earn royalties based on the number of minutes watched by premium members.

Best For: Educators and creatives.

<u>Amazon Kindle Direct Publishing (KDP)</u>

How It Works: Self-publish eBooks and paperbacks. Earn royalties from book sales.

Best For: Authors and writers.

<u>Gumroad</u>

How It Works: Sell digital products like eBooks, music, videos, and software. Earn money from each sale.

Best For: Creators of digital content.

<u>Sellfy</u>

How It Works: Sell digital products, subscriptions, and print-on-demand merchandise. Earn money from each sale.

Best For: Digital product creators and artists.

<u>Etsy</u>

How It Works: Sell digital downloads such as printable art, planners, and other creative assets. Earn money from each sale.

Best For: Creatives and designers.

<u>Creative Market</u>

How It Works: Sell digital design assets like fonts, graphics, and templates. Earn money from each sale.

Best For: Graphic designers and artists.

<u>Redbubble</u>

How It Works: Upload your designs and earn a commission on sales of print-on-demand products featuring your designs.

Best For: Artists and graphic designers.

<u>Shutterstock / Adobe Stock</u>

How It Works: Upload photos, videos, and other digital assets. Earn royalties each time your content is downloaded.

Best For: Photographers and videographers.

Anchor

How It Works: Create podcasts and monetize through sponsorships and listener donations.

Best For: Podcasters.

Pond5

How It Works: Sell stock videos, music, sound effects, and other media. Earn royalties from each sale.

Best For: Videographers and musicians.

Envato Market

How It Works: Sell digital assets on various marketplaces (e.g., ThemeForest for themes, AudioJungle for music). Earn money from each sale.

Best For: Web developers, graphic designers, and musicians.

Blurb

How It Works: Create and sell high-quality photo books, trade books, and magazines. Earn money from each sale.

Best For: Photographers and authors.

Podia

How It Works: Sell online courses, memberships, and digital downloads. Earn money from each sale.

Best For: Educators and digital product creators.

Thinkific

How It Works: Create and sell online courses. Thinkific offers various tools for course creation and marketing.

Best For: Educators and course creators.

By leveraging these platforms, you can generate passive income from your content creation efforts across various mediums, whether it's writing, video, audio, digital art, or educational content.

We have already looked at my experience with Amazon KDP and Etsy. I have built up passive income streams from both of these methods of content creation.

Over the next few chapters, we will look more closely at making courses, stock photography, blogging, and vlogging. I have tried most of these methods of content creation whilst pursuing my passive income dream and I am hoping that hearing about my experiences might be useful.

Key points:

As always, what you get out in terms of financial reward will depend upon how hard you work as well as the quality of your content.

Consistency is key.

Additionally:

In the field of content creation, you don't have to do all of the work yourself.

AI can help speed up your workflow, and there are hundreds of freelancers out there willing to help you with your projects.

We will look at outsourcing and the utilisation of AI later in the book.

Making and selling courses

A recent trend in the world of passive income/content creation/ selling digital products is the making and selling of courses.

I have personally kept away from this arena, and I shall tell you why.

My social media, like yours I am sure, has been flooded with sponsored adverts for digital courses. The main topic that these courses seem to be teaching is how to make and sell courses.

You can also buy templates for making courses, and indeed ready-made courses that you can edit and sell as your own.

Now, I am sure that it is possible to make a great passive income from selling courses about such things as how to make courses. However, here is a little story that has prevented me from either buying or making any type of course whatsoever.

I was reading an interesting forum on the Threads platform. This is an extension of Instagram and a place for people to discuss topics of every nature possible.

The forum that I accidentally stumbled upon was about, drum roll, courses that teach people how to make money from selling digital files. Someone had posted that they had sold a few of their courses but hadn't managed to sell a single one of the digital files that she had made and put up for sale.

So people are creating courses about endeavours in which they have had no success whatsoever. What they are offering is (sometimes/often) regurgitated courses telling people how to make money when they have failed at whatever it is they are teaching.

There are hundreds of course writing gurus out there, but is what they are telling you to do sourced from personal experience? In many cases, I believe not. In any case, the world of courses seems to be oversaturated. I do not want to put you off this option for making a passive income. Indeed, if you have something to teach, you can find numerous free templates in which to present your course. The superb graphic design platform Canva is one example.

However, I honestly think that a course will only work if you have genuine knowledge and experience about your topic. For example, if you are brilliant at decorating cakes. This might well work because you can show examples of your work and then teach people either by video or photos how to recreate what you have done.

I would however personally avoid making courses about making courses or teaching something about which you have little knowledge or in which you have seen little success.

It would be like me writing a book about making a passive income when I hadn't made any money that way myself.

Anyway, if you fancy having a go at making courses, here is some interesting information for you.

You can sell courses that you create yourself on several popular online platforms designed specifically for course creators. Here are some of the top options:

<u>Udemy</u>

Overview: Udemy is one of the largest online learning platforms with millions of students worldwide.

Pros: Large audience, marketing support, easy-to-use interface.

Cons: Udemy takes a significant percentage of course sales, and there are restrictions on pricing and promotions.

Teachable

Overview: Teachable allows you to create and sell your courses and provides a customizable platform.

Pros: Full control over branding, pricing, and student data, integrated with various marketing tools.

Cons: Monthly subscription fees and transaction fees on the free plan.

Thinkific

Overview: Thinkific offers a platform for creating, marketing, and selling online courses.

Pros: Easy to use, customizable, supports various types of content (videos, quizzes, assignments).

Cons: Pricing plans can be expensive for advanced features, and limited marketing tools compared to others.

Kajabi

Overview: Kajabi is an all-in-one platform for creating and selling online courses, memberships, and other digital products.

Pros: Comprehensive marketing tools, customizable, supports memberships and community features.

Cons: High monthly cost, steep learning curve for beginners.

Skillshare

Overview: Skillshare focuses on creative and educational content and operates on a subscription model.

Pros: Access to a large community of learners, potential for recurring revenue through royalties.

Cons: Payment based on watch time, less control over pricing and course structure.

<u>Podia</u>

Overview: Podia offers a platform for selling online courses, digital downloads, and memberships.

Pros: No transaction fees, easy to use, integrates with email marketing tools.

Cons: Limited customization options, and fewer marketing tools compared to other platforms.

<u>Coursera</u>

Overview: Coursera partners with universities and organizations to offer courses, certifications, and degrees.

Pros: Access to a large, global audience, strong reputation.

<u>Mighty Networks</u>

Overview: Mighty Networks allows you to create a community-based platform where you can sell courses.

Pros: Community engagement features, support courses, and memberships.

Cons: More focused on community building, might be less suitable if you only want to sell courses.

<u>Gumroad</u>

Overview: Gumroad is a platform for selling digital products, including online courses.

Pros: Simple to use, low transaction fees, good for small creators.

Cons: Limited features compared to dedicated course platforms.

<u>LearnWorlds</u>

Overview: LearnWorlds offers a robust platform for creating, marketing, and selling online courses.

Pros: Highly customizable, interactive features, supports various content formats.

Cons: Pricing plans can be expensive, steep learning curve for advanced customization requirements (e.g., control over pricing, need for marketing tools, audience reach),

You can choose the platform that best fits your goals.

So how do you go about making a course?

Creating a course designed to generate passive income involves several key steps, from planning and development to marketing and sales. Here's a structured approach to get you started:

<u>Identify Your Niche and Audience</u>

Find Your Niche: Choose a topic you're knowledgeable and passionate about. Ensure there's a demand by researching what people are searching for online. The website Google Trends is a good place to check out the popularity of a keyword or topic. You can also simply type a query into Google's search bar. The autocomplete suggestions will give you a good idea about what people are looking for.

Define Your Audience: Identify your target audience, their needs, and pain points. Understand what they want to learn and how they prefer to learn it.

Validate Your Course Idea

Market Research: Check platforms like Udemy, Teachable, and forums to see if similar courses exist and their popularity.

Plan Your Course Content

Outline Your Course: Break down the topic into modules and lessons. Create a detailed course outline covering all key points.

Learning Objectives: Define clear learning outcome

Surveys and Feedback: Conduct surveys or interviews with potential students to gauge interest and gather feedback on each module and lesson.

Resources and Materials: Gather or create necessary resources, such as PDFs, worksheets, and supplementary materials.

Create the Course

Content Creation: Record video lectures, write scripts, create slides, and design additional materials.

Quality Production: Invest in good equipment (camera, microphone, lighting) to ensure high-quality video and audio. Use screen recording software if needed.

Editing: Edit your videos to ensure clarity and engagement. Use software like Adobe Premiere Pro, Final Cut Pro, or simpler tools like Camtasia.

Choose a Platform

Course Hosting: Select a platform to host your course (e.g., Udemy, Teachable, Thinkific, Podia - see previous list in this chapter). Compare features, pricing, and ease of use.

Pricing Strategy: Decide on your course pricing. Consider offering different tiers or bundles.

<u>Market Your Course</u>

- Create a Landing Page: Design a compelling landing page with clear information about the course, benefits, testimonials, and a call to action.

- SEO and Content Marketing: Optimise your landing page for search engines. Start a blog or YouTube channel to drive organic traffic.

- Email Marketing: Build an email list and use it to promote your course. Offer lead magnets (free content) to attract subscribers.

- Social Media Marketing: Leverage social media platforms to reach your audience. Use paid ads if necessary to boost visibility.

- Partnerships and Affiliates: Collaborate with influencers, bloggers, and other course creators to promote your course.

<u>Launch Your Course</u>

- Pre-Launch: Build anticipation with teasers, webinars, and special offers. Engage with your audience through email and social media.

- Launch: Announce your course, offer limited-time discounts, and encourage students to enrol.

Gather Feedback and Improve

- Student Feedback: Collect feedback from students to understand what's working and what needs improvement.

- Course Updates: Regularly update your course content based on feedback and industry changes to keep it relevant.

Automate and Scale

- Automation Tools: Use tools to automate email marketing, customer support, and sales funnels.

- Scalability: Create additional courses or expand existing ones to cover more topics within your niche.

Monitor and Optimise

- Analytics: Monitor course performance through platform analytics and feedback.

- Continuous Improvement: Regularly update and refine your marketing strategies, course content, and user experience.

By following these steps, you can create a high-quality course that meets the needs of your audience and generates passive income.

Course creation, as with most things mentioned in this book, requires upfront effort and investment, but once your course is up and running, it can provide a steady stream of passive income with minimal ongoing effort.

Please do not let me deter you from entering the field of course creation. It is just an area that has never appealed to me personally, I think I prefer to sit and write a book old-school style.

Stock photography

Stock photography refers to a collection of photographs that are licensed for specific uses. These photos are typically pre-shot and made available through stock photography websites for purchase or free download. They can be used for various purposes, such as in advertisements, websites, blogs, presentations, and other media.

The key characteristics of stock photography:

- Pre-Shot and Pre-Edited: The photos are taken and edited by photographers before being uploaded to stock photography websites.

- Licensing: Photos are sold or made available under different licensing agreements, such as royalty-free or rights-managed.

- Versatility: Stock photos cover a wide range of subjects, themes, and styles to meet diverse needs.

- Accessibility: They are readily available for immediate download and use, making them a convenient resource for designers, marketers, and content creators.

Types of stock photography:

Royalty-Free

- Allows buyers to use the photo multiple times for a single fee without paying royalties for each use.

- There are still some restrictions, such as not being able to resell the image as part of another product.

Rights-Managed (RM)

- Requires buyers to pay for each specific use of the photo.

- Licensing fees are determined by factors such as duration, geographic location, and intended use.

- Provides more control over the photo's use and can limit its distribution to avoid oversaturation.

Microstock

- Typically lower-cost stock photos available through microstock agencies.

- Usually sold under royalty-free licences.

- Ideal for small businesses, bloggers, and individuals with limited budgets.

This is how stock photography works:

- Photographers: Capture and edit photos, then upload them to stock photography websites.

- Stock Photography Websites: Platforms like Shutterstock, Adobe Stock, Getty Images, and iStock serve as marketplaces for these photos.

- Buyers: Purchase licences to use the photos for various purposes. They can search for images based on keywords, categories, or styles.

● Licensing Agreements: Define the terms of use for each photo, including any restrictions on usage.

How to earn a passive income from stock photography:

● Upload to Multiple Platforms: Increase exposure and potential sales by uploading your photos to various stock photography websites.

● High-Quality Images: Focus on producing high-quality, high-resolution images that are well-composed and professionally edited.

● Diverse Portfolio: Capture a wide range of subjects and themes to appeal to different buyers.

● Keyword Optimization: Use relevant and specific keywords to make your photos easily searchable.

● Regular Updates: Continuously add new photos to keep your portfolio fresh and increase your chances of sales.

● Trends and Demand: Keep an eye on current trends and popular themes to capture photos that are in high demand.

Here are the most popular stock photography platforms:

1. Shutterstock

2. Adobe Stock

3. Getty Images

4. iStock

5. Alamy

6. Depositphotos

7. Pond5

8. 123RF

9. Dreamstime

10. Bigstock

Stock photography provides a convenient and cost-effective way for buyers to access high-quality images while allowing photographers to earn passive income by licensing their work.

I hold a portfolio of photographs with Adobe Stock. I think this is the best agency to deal with. The payment per sale is generally higher than the other two main agencies, Shutterstock and Getty/IStock.

I am a hobby photographer, and professional photographers are bound to make more income than I do because of the quality of their photos.

I repeatedly images of my melanoma skin cancer before it was removed. I spent the time to get some decent photos of it with good lighting, and I used a DSLR camera.

These photos are useful to anyone writing articles about skin disorders, cancer or melanoma, and therefore I receive royalties every time someone licences one of the images.

Adobe Stock allows creators to upload photographs, illustrations, video clips, and music. Customers (usually other creators) licence them and the original maker receives a royalty.

What may interest someone who is not an artist or photographer is that Adobe Stock now offers AI imagery for licensing. This has brought about a surge of new contributors, all making art from word prompts via software such as Adobe Firefly.

There is an argument that the images produced by AI are nothing but stolen artwork.

The question of whether AI-generated images constitute "stolen artwork" is complex and depends on various factors, including how the AI was trained, the sources of the training data, and the legal and ethical considerations surrounding AI and copyright. Here's a detailed overview of the key issues:

How AI-Generated Images Are Created

1. Training Data: AI models, particularly those for generating images (like GANs or diffusion models), are trained on large datasets containing images. These datasets can include a wide variety of images from different sources.

2. Algorithms: The AI learns patterns, styles, and features from these images and uses this knowledge to generate new images.

Key Issues

1. Source of Training Data:

- Licensed or Public Domain: If the AI is trained on images that are licensed for such use or are in the public domain, the resulting images are less likely to raise ethical or legal concerns.

- Unlicensed Use: If the AI is trained on copyrighted images without permission from the copyright holders, this can be problematic. The creators of the AI or the datasets might not have the right to use these images for training.

2. Copyright Infringement:

- Direct Copying: If an AI generates an image that is a direct copy of a copyrighted work, it would infringe on the original artist's rights.

- Derivative Works: If the AI generates images that are significantly similar to specific copyrighted works, these could be considered derivative works, which may also infringe on copyright.

3. Transformative Use:

-Fair Use Doctrine: In some jurisdictions, creating new works that are transformative (significantly different from the original and adding new expression or meaning) may be considered fair use. Whether AI-generated images qualify as transformative is still a gray area in legal terms.

Ethical Considerations

1. Artists' Rights: Artists may feel that their work is being exploited if their images are used without consent to train AI models, especially if those models generate images that compete with the artists' original works.

2. Attribution and Compensation: There is an ongoing debate about whether artists whose work is used to train AI should be attributed or compensated for their contributions.

Legal Landscape

The legal status of AI-generated images varies by jurisdiction and is still evolving. Some important points include:

- Copyright Law: Many copyright laws do not explicitly address AI-generated content. Courts and lawmakers are still determining how existing laws apply to AI.

- Moral Rights: In some countries, artists have moral rights, which include the right to be credited for their work and to object to derogatory treatments of it.

<u>Best Practices</u>

For developers and users of AI-generated images, some best practices include:

- Transparency: Being transparent about how the AI is trained and what data sources are used.

- Seeking Permission: Where possible, seeking permission from artists or using legally licensed or public domain images for training AI models.

- Respecting Copyright: Ensuring that the generated images do not infringe on the copyrights of existing works.

So while AI-generated images themselves are not inherently "stolen artwork," the process of creating them can involve ethical and legal issues, especially concerning the use of copyrighted material for training.

The debate is ongoing, and clear guidelines and regulations are still being developed. Until then, those involved in AI image generation should strive to respect the rights of original artists and adhere to legal and ethical standards.

Complex, indeed. However, people are creating imagery (and indeed many other forms of content) via AI and using this to contribute to their passive income, and this is an option available to you should you be able to or care to learn to use prompts to make licensable photographs and illustrations.

Adobe Stock has established clear guidelines regarding the submission of AI-generated imagery, which reflect its efforts to ensure quality and originality while navigating the complex legal and ethical landscape associated with AI content. Here's a detailed look at Adobe Stock's stance and requirements:

<u>Acceptance Criteria for AI-Generated Images</u>

1. Transparency and Disclosure:

- Adobe Stock requires contributors to disclose if an image was created using AI. This transparency helps maintain trust and ensures that buyers are aware of the origin of the content.

2. Quality Standards:

- AI-generated images must meet the same quality standards as other submissions. This includes high resolution, appropriate composition, and technical excellence (e.g., proper lighting, focus, and lack of artifacts).

3. Originality and Uniqueness:

- Adobe Stock emphasises the need for original and unique content. AI-generated images should not be mere reproductions or slight modifications of existing works. They should bring new and creative perspectives.

4. Compliance with Legal Requirements:

- Contributors must ensure that their AI-generated images do not infringe on any copyrights or intellectual property rights. This means the training data used to create the AI model should not include unlicensed, copyrighted material.

5. Ethical Use of AI:

- Adobe Stock encourages the ethical use of AI technology, respecting the rights of original creators and avoiding the creation of misleading or deceptive content.

<u>Specific Guidelines for AI-Generated Content</u>

1. Model and Property Releases:

- If AI-generated images include recognizable human figures or elements that could require a property release (such as recognizable landmarks or branded objects), contributors must ensure that appropriate releases are obtained, just as with traditional photography.

2. Avoiding Misrepresentation:

- Contributors should avoid submitting AI-generated images that could be easily mistaken for real photographs unless clearly labelled. This helps prevent any potential misrepresentation or confusion among buyers.

3. Metadata and Keywords:

- Proper metadata and keywords must be included to accurately describe AI-generated images. This ensures that buyers can find and understand the context of the images they are purchasing.

<u>Review Process</u>

Adobe Stock employs a rigorous review process for all submissions, including AI-generated imagery. Each submission is evaluated based on the aforementioned criteria. If an image fails to meet Adobe's standards or guidelines, it may be rejected.

Adobe Stock is committed to integrating AI-generated content into its portfolio while maintaining high standards of quality, originality, and legal compliance. Contributors who wish to submit AI-generated images to Adobe Stock should:

1. Be Transparent: Clearly disclose the AI origin of the images.

2. Ensure Quality: Adhere to Adobe's quality standards.

3. Respect Intellectual Property: Use legally obtained training data and avoid infringing on copyrights.

4. Follow Ethical Guidelines: Respect the rights of original creators and provide accurate representations.

By following these guidelines, contributors can successfully submit AI-generated imagery to Adobe Stock, enriching the platform's diverse collection of creative content.

I have personally tried to upload some AI imagery to Adobe Stock. What can I say, I like to try things out. Most have been rejected for quality issues, and of the ones that have been accepted the download count is very low.

I think that making a passive income from stock photography is difficult due to the extremely high number of submissions from creators, especially now that AI imagery is allowed.

However, if you have a talent for photography, illustration, or videography, and you take the time to learn about what sort of work is in demand for licensing - in other words, useful content - it is possible to build up a very good passive income stream from stock.

Please note that AI-generated work is not accepted by Shutterstock or Getty at present, just Adobe Stock. This may change over time.

Blogging

Blogging is the act of writing and publishing content on a blog, which is a website or section of a website that features regularly updated posts or articles. These posts are typically written in an informal or conversational style and cover a wide range of topics, depending on the interests and expertise of the blogger. Here's a detailed overview of blogging:

<u>Key Components of Blogging:</u>

1. Blog Posts:

- Individual articles or entries published on a blog.

- Can include text, images, videos, infographics, and other media.

- Usually displayed in reverse chronological order (newest posts first).

2. Topics and Niches:

- Bloggers often focus on specific topics or niches such as travel, food, fashion, technology, personal finance, health, or personal experiences.

- Choosing a niche helps attract a dedicated audience interested in that subject.

3. Audience Engagement:

- Successful blogs engage with their readers through comments, social media, email newsletters, and other interactive features.

- Building a community around a blog is key to its growth and sustainability.

<u>Steps to Start Blogging:</u>

1. Choose a Blogging Platform:

- WordPress.org: Self-hosted option offering full control and customization.

- WordPress.com: Hosted service with more limited options but easier to start. I use this platform for my knitting blog.

- Blogger: Google's free blogging platform.

- Medium: Platform for writers, offering a built-in audience and simple interface.

- Wix, Squarespace: Website builders that include blogging features.

2. Select a Domain Name and Hosting:

- Domain Name: The web address (e.g., www.yourblogname.com).

- Hosting: Service that stores your blog's files and makes them accessible online. Options include Bluehost, SiteGround, and others for self-hosted blogs.

3. Design Your Blog:

- Choose a theme or template that matches your style and niche.

- Customise the design to create a unique look and improve user experience.

4. Create Quality Content:

- Write engaging, informative, and valuable posts that resonate with your target audience.

- Use multimedia (images, videos) to enhance your posts.

- Optimise for SEO (Search Engine Optimization) to increase visibility in search engines.

5. Promote Your Blog:

- Share your posts on social media platforms (Facebook, Twitter, Instagram, Pinterest).

- Engage with readers through comments and social media interactions.

- Collaborate with other bloggers and participate in blogging communities.

6. How to Monetise Your Blog :

- Advertising: Use ad networks like Google AdSense or direct ad sales.

- Affiliate Marketing: Promote products or services and earn a commission on sales.

- Sponsored Posts: Write posts for brands in exchange for payment.

- Sell Products/Services: Offer digital products (eBooks, courses) or services (consulting, coaching).

- Subscription Models: Offer premium content or membership for a fee.

<u>Benefits of Blogging:</u>

1. Self-Expression and Creativity: Blogging provides a platform for sharing your thoughts, ideas, and experiences.

2. Building Expertise and Authority: Regularly writing about a specific topic can establish you as an expert in that field.

3. Networking Opportunities: Engaging with readers and other bloggers can lead to valuable connections and collaborations.

4. Potential Income: With consistent effort and the right monetization strategies, blogging can become a source of passive income.

5. Personal Development: Blogging improves writing skills, discipline, and knowledge about your chosen topic.

<u>Challenges of Blogging:</u>

1. Time and Effort: Maintaining a successful blog requires regular content creation, promotion, and engagement.

2. Consistency: Posting regularly and maintaining quality can be challenging.

3. Competition: With millions of blogs online, standing out requires unique content and effective marketing strategies.

4. Technical Aspects: Managing a blog involves understanding basic web design, SEO, and other technical skills.

Overall, blogging is a versatile and accessible way to share information, connect with others, and potentially earn a great passive income. It combines creativity, communication, and digital literacy, making it a valuable endeavour for individuals and businesses alike.

I started a blog during the lockdown. The topic is knitting, I call it a 'knitting magazine'.

Some people believe that blogging is dead, that people these days prefer to watch videos for information and do not want to spend time reading articles.

I disagree. I think the older generation (including myself) prefers reading over watching videos. This excludes visual learners of course. But surely I am not alone in choosing an article over a video when I want to find out how something is done or discover more information about a topic of interest.

I chose to use the platform Wordpress.com for my blog. You can sign up to this platform for free. I chose a paid package because this includes an easy way to show adverts and therefore make a passive income.

My website/blog receives about 60,000 views per year. Let us look at whether or not this constitutes a successful blog:

Determining what constitutes a "successful" blog in terms of annual visits can vary widely depending on the blog's goals, niche, and the blogger's personal expectations. However, some general benchmarks can help gauge success:

General Benchmarks for Blog Success

- Small/Personal Blogs: For personal or hobby blogs, a few thousand visits per month (or around 30,000-50,000 visits per year) might be considered successful.

- Niche Blogs: For blogs in specific niches (e.g., tech, travel, health), reaching 50,000-100,000 visits per year could indicate a successful blog, as these niches often have more targeted and engaged audiences.

- Professional/Business Blogs: For blogs aiming to generate significant income or support a business, 100,000-500,000 visits per year or more might be a common target.

I would say my blog is not quite there in terms of success. I have found blogging to be a very slow and time-consuming process. I do make a small passive income from it, however, the blog itself costs around 100 pounds a year so at first I saw a financial deficit.

The income I make from my blog is mostly via affiliate links. I will write an article about my favourite yarn, for example. Some of the yarn types will be connected to a link, and if someone clicks on this link and then makes a purchase I will receive a commission.

As you would imagine, people working on a blog full-time may well be able to reach very high levels of passive income earning. A successful travel blogger, for example, who earns commission from holiday sales, could receive hundreds from just one person purchasing via their affiliate link. Scale this up and you are looking at a very nice lifestyle via passive income.

My blog is most definitely an example of not spending enough time tending to my garden. I don't write anywhere near enough articles, and my affiliate links are mostly for low-ticket items such as knitting patterns and balls of wool. I think that blogging is quite hard work as you have to keep your website current and have a stream of new ideas.

I think I have too many irons on the fire and am a jack of all trades. This causes burnout and I think that sometimes too many passive dreams are a bad idea. I would try blogging if you love writing articles, have a passion for a topic and won't struggle to find new things to write about.

Blogging is known to be a prolonged burn in terms of building a passive income. Generally, you shouldn't expect to make anything for the first two or three years. However, some bloggers have made millions. They work hard, with consistency, producing content that their followers eagerly read. Successful bloggers turn themselves into authoritative and trustworthy sources of information about a topic, so much so that people will go on and buy products from their recommendations.

I do recommend Wordpress.com to a new blogger and would like to use the rest of this chapter to tell you more about this platform.

What is WordPress.com

WordPress.com is a hosted blogging platform that allows users to create and manage blogs or websites without needing to deal with the technical aspects of hosting, security, and maintenance. It's a service provided by Automattic, the company founded by one of the original developers of the open-source WordPress software.

How WordPress.com Works

Creating an Account

- Sign Up: To start using WordPress.com, you need to sign up for an account. This involves choosing a username, password, and email address.

- Choose a Plan**: WordPress.com offers several plans, including a free option and various paid plans with additional features.

Setting Up Your Blog or Website

- Select a Domain: On the free plan, your site will have a WordPress.com subdomain (e.g., yoursite.wordpress.com). Paid plans allow you to use a custom domain (e.g., yoursite.com). I use a paid plan and I have my .com domain.

- Choose a Theme: WordPress.com provides a variety of themes that determine the appearance of your site. You can browse and select a theme that fits your style or niche.

- Customise Your Site: Use the customization options to adjust colours, fonts, layouts, and other design elements. Paid plans offer more advanced customization options.

Creating Content

- Posts and Pages: You can create blog posts (regularly updated content) and pages (static content, such as an About or Contact page).

- Block Editor: WordPress.com uses the Gutenberg block editor, which allows you to create content using blocks for text, images, videos, galleries, and more.

- Media Library: Upload and manage images, videos, and other media files that you want to include in your posts and pages.

Publishing and Managing Content

- Publish: Once your content is ready, you can publish it immediately or schedule it for a future date and time.

- Categories and Tags: Organize your content using categories and tags, making it easier for visitors to navigate your site and find relevant posts.

- Comments: Enable comments to engage with your readers. WordPress.com provides tools for moderating and managing comments.

Site Management

- Dashboard: The WordPress.com dashboard is your control center for managing your site. From here, you can create content, customise your site, view stats, and manage settings.

● Plugins and Widgets: While plugin use is limited on WordPress.com compared to self-hosted WordPress.org, higher-tier plans offer access to a selection of plugins and widgets to extend site functionality.

● SEO Tools: Paid plans include SEO tools to help optimise your site for search engines.

● Analytics: WordPress.com provides built-in analytics to track your site's traffic, visitor behaviour, and other key metrics.

Key Features of WordPress.com

● Ease of Use: Ideal for beginners, WordPress.com handles hosting, security, and updates, allowing you to focus on content creation.

● Scalability: Suitable for small personal blogs to more complex websites, with various plans to accommodate different needs.

● Themes and Customization: Access to a wide range of themes and customization options to create a unique site.

● Community and Support: Extensive documentation, community forums, and customer support (with paid plans) to assist users.

Differences Between WordPress.com and WordPress.org

- Hosting: WordPress.com is a hosted service, whereas WordPress.org is self-hosted, requiring you to arrange your web hosting.

- Customization: WordPress.org offers more extensive customization options and plugin support, whereas WordPress.com has restrictions, especially on lower-tier plans.

- Control: With WordPress.org, you have full control over your site and its data. WordPress.com manages many aspects for you, providing less control but more convenience.

WordPress.com is a powerful platform for creating and managing websites and blogs, especially for users who prefer a hassle-free setup and maintenance experience. It offers various plans to suit different needs, from personal blogs to business websites, with a focus on ease of use, security, and reliability.

If you plump for a paid plan, you can easily monetise your content via advertising. It is just a matter of signing up for the built-in advertising programme. Unlike with some advertising platforms, you will be paid just for advertisement display and not via the number of clicks. The more people visit your blog, the more money potential there is.

Some other blogging platforms were mentioned earlier in this chapter. As always, please go check them out. Most have a free option so you can have a play and see if the pricing and way each one works is manageable for you.

Vlogging

Vlogging, short for "video blogging," involves creating and sharing video content on various platforms, primarily YouTube, but also on Vimeo, Instagram, TikTok, Facebook, and other social media sites. Vloggers document their lives, share their expertise, or entertain their audience through videos, which can range from daily life updates to tutorials, reviews, and more.

Vlogging is another way that you make a passive income from the content that you create. I have recently started vlogging on the YouTube platform. As always, I was interested to see how it all works and how easy or not it is to make money in this manner.

Answer - nothing is easy. Vlogging, like any other passive income method, takes time, consistency, hard work, and talent. You need 1000 subscribers and a huge amount of viewing hours before you can even apply to receive payments for advertising.

A couple of my videos have adverts on them already (I only started a month ago) and yet I will not receive a penny from this - it all goes to YouTube. I didn't know this and always assumed that all advertising revenue went to the video creators. Not the case.

Anyway, here is a guide about where you should start if you are interested in vlogging and making a passive income from this field.

<u>Steps to Start Vlogging</u>

1. Choose Your Niche:

- Identify a specific topic or area of interest that you are passionate about and knowledgeable in. Popular niches include travel, tech reviews, beauty, fitness, food, and lifestyle.

2. Set Up Your Equipment:

- Camera: A good quality camera or smartphone.

- Microphone: To ensure clear audio.

- Lighting: Natural light or affordable lighting kits to improve video quality.

- Editing Software: Software like Adobe Premiere Pro, Final Cut Pro, or free options like iMovie and DaVinci Resolve.

3. Create Content:

- Plan your videos, create a content calendar, and script or outline your videos to stay organised.

- Film and edit your videos to ensure they are engaging and of high quality.

4. Upload and Optimise:

- Upload your videos to your chosen platform(s).

- Optimise your video titles, descriptions, and tags for SEO to increase visibility.

- Create eye-catching thumbnails to attract viewers.

5. Promote Your Videos:

- Share your videos on social media, in relevant online communities, and through email newsletters to drive traffic.

- Engage with your audience by responding to comments and interacting with viewers.

<u>How to Make Passive Income from Vlogging</u>

1. Ad Revenue:

- YouTube Partner Program: Once you meet YouTube's requirements (1,000 subscribers and 4,000 watch hours in the past 12 months), you can monetize your channel with ads. You earn money based on ad views and clicks.

- Other Platforms: Some other platforms like Facebook and Instagram also offer monetization options through ads.

2. Affiliate Marketing:

- Promote products or services in your videos and include affiliate links in your video descriptions. You earn a commission for each sale made through your links. Popular affiliate programs include Amazon Associates, ShareASale, and Commission Junction (discussed fully in a previous chapter).

3. Sponsorships and Brand Deals:

- Partner with brands to create sponsored content. Brands pay you to promote their products or services in your videos. The amount you can charge depends on your audience size and engagement rates.

4. Merchandise Sales:

- Create and sell your own branded merchandise (t-shirts, mugs, etc.) through platforms like Teespring, Merch by Amazon, or Shopify. Promote your merchandise in your videos and provide purchase links.

5. Crowdfunding and Donations:

- Use platforms like Patreon, Ko-fi, or Buy Me a Coffee to receive financial support from your audience. Offer exclusive content, early access to videos, or other perks to your supporters.

6. Digital Products:

- Create and sell digital products such as eBooks, online courses, presets, or templates. Promote these products in your videos and provide links for purchase. I shall be doing this with this book that you are reading to see what happens.

7. Membership Programs:

- Offer a membership program through platforms like YouTube Memberships or Patreon, where subscribers pay a monthly fee for exclusive content, live streams, and other benefits.

<u>Tips for Building a Successful Vlogging Channel</u>

1. Consistency: Regularly upload content to keep your audience engaged and attract new viewers.

2. Quality: Focus on producing high-quality videos with good visuals and clear audio.

3. Engagement: Interact with your audience by responding to comments and asking for feedback.

4. SEO: Optimise your videos for search engines to increase visibility and attract more viewers.

5. Promotion: Actively promote your videos on social media and other platforms to reach a wider audience.

Vlogging offers multiple avenues for generating passive income, primarily through ad revenue, affiliate marketing, sponsorships, merchandise sales, and more.

The key to success in vlogging lies in creating high-quality, engaging content, building a loyal audience, and effectively monetizing your channel through various strategies. With dedication and strategic effort, vlogging can become a lucrative source of passive income.

Hiring freelancers

As mentioned before, if you are looking to make a passive income via content creation, you can speed up the process by hiring freelancers to do some work for you.

Fiverr is an example of a platform where you can find talented people willing to help you out with a multitude of diverse projects.

I have used Fiverr myself. I hired a woman from Pakistan to write some articles for my knitting blog. I like to think that I was helping out a young student (that is how she described herself) and I gave her a nice tip. The articles themselves were satisfactory. I tend to always prefer to do my writing but I was very busy and at that time was quite into the blog and decided to invest in some genuinely passive work.

The only drawback really with hiring freelancers (apart from the cost of course) is finding the right people. There is an entire army of talented folk out there. All you can do is spend time reading reviews and looking at portfolios of previous work, if these are available.

My brother is a musician and he uses the Fiverr platform regularly. He buys backing vocals and unusual music samples. For example, he recently wrote a song called 'Just Like William Shakespeare" and he found a specialist in playing mediaeval instruments to add some authenticity to his track.

I have only ever used Fiverr to find freelancers and have therefore exclusively written about this platform. There are, as you would expect, numerous places where you can find freelancers for content creation beyond Fiverr. Here are some popular ones:

1. Upwork: A large freelancing platform where you can find professionals in various fields, including content creation, writing, graphic design, and more.

2. Freelancer.com: Similar to Upwork, this platform allows you to post jobs and receive bids from freelancers around the world.

3. Toptal: This platform connects you with top freelancers in various industries, including content creators, writers, and designers. Toptal is known for its rigorous screening process.

4. Guru: Another freelancing platform where you can find a wide range of professionals for your content creation needs.

5. PeoplePerHour: This platform allows you to hire freelancers by the hour or for specific projects, making it flexible for various types of content creation work.

6. 99designs: Specialising in design work, you can find graphic designers to create visual content for your projects.

7. Contena: Focused specifically on writers and content creators, Contena helps you find experienced freelance writers and editors.

8. Textbroker: A platform specifically for finding freelance writers. You can order content at different quality levels and prices.

9. WriterAccess: Another platform focused on content creation, where you can find writers, editors, and content strategists.

10. Contently: This platform connects brands with freelance content creators, including writers, photographers, and videographers.

11. Scripted: Focused on writing, Scripted allows you to hire freelance writers for various types of content, including blog posts, articles, and social media content.

12. CloudPeeps: A platform that connects you with freelance marketers, including content creators and social media managers.

13. ProBlogger Job Board: A job board specifically for finding professional bloggers and writers.

14. SimplyHired: A job search engine where you can post freelance content creation jobs and search for freelance talent.

Each of these platforms has its strengths and can cater to different types of content creation needs. Consider the specific requirements of your project and the type of freelancer you need when choosing a platform.

Using AI to help make a passive income

———

We have already touched on the topic of using AI to help make a passive income in the field of stock photography.

AI can be a powerful tool in creating content that generates passive income in many other ways:

1. Content Creation and Curation

- Blog Posts and Articles: AI can generate high-quality articles and blog posts on various topics. Tools like OpenAI's GPT-4 can produce well-researched and coherent content that can attract traffic and ad revenue.

- Ebooks AI can help write, edit, and format ebooks. These can be sold on platforms like Amazon Kindle Direct Publishing.

- Social Media Content: AI can create engaging posts for social media platforms, helping grow an audience and driving traffic to monetized sites.

2. SEO Optimization:

- Keyword Research: AI tools can identify profitable keywords and phrases that can improve the search engine ranking of your content.

- Content Optimization: AI can suggest improvements to your content to enhance readability and SEO performance, ensuring it reaches a wider audience.

3. Video and Audio Content:

- Scriptwriting: AI can generate scripts for YouTube videos, podcasts, and other video content.

- Video Editing: AI tools can assist in editing videos, adding subtitles, and improving video quality.

- Voiceover*: AI-generated voices can be used for narration in videos and podcasts.

4. Email Marketing:

- Email Drafting: AI can craft personalised and engaging email content for marketing campaigns.

- Automation: AI can manage email lists and automate email sequences to nurture leads and convert them into paying customers.

5. Course Creation:

- Content Development: AI can help develop the curriculum and create course materials for online courses, which can be sold on platforms like Udemy or Teachable.

- Interactive Content: AI can create quizzes, assignments, and interactive content to enhance the learning experience.

6. Data Analysis:

- Performance Tracking: AI can analyse the performance of your content, identifying what works best and providing insights for future content strategies.

- Audience Insights: AI can help understand your audience better, allowing for more targeted and effective content creation.

7. Graphic Design:

- Image and Video Creation: AI tools can generate images, infographics, and even videos that complement your content, making it more visually appealing.

- Logo and Branding: AI can assist in creating professional logos and branding materials.

8. Affiliate Marketing:

- Content for Affiliate Sites: AI can generate product reviews, comparisons, and other content that can drive affiliate sales.

- Product Recommendations: AI can personalise product recommendations based on user behaviour and preferences.

By leveraging AI in these areas, you can create a steady stream of high-quality content that attracts traffic and generates revenue over time, contributing to a sustainable passive income.

Some of this book has been written with the help of AI. I used ChatGPT to help with ideas and information, and then I went in and edited the information that was generated.

Using AI in self-published books is accepted, as long as you are open and upfront about it. When uploading to Amazon, you will be asked whether and to what extent you have used AI. I think it is always best to answer honestly because Amazon is well known for simply vanishing entire accounts when people do not stick to the guidelines.

There are of course ethical issues around using AI. How is such content generated? Does the fake brain simply copy other people's work, and what it generates is therefore plagiarism? Because of such unanswered questions, I think that when you use AI, you do need to carefully edit and adjust whatever content you have been given.

Make the work of AI into your original content. Let us compare using AI with writing an academic essay. When I was at university for example, I would pore over research books and use the information therein to formulate my arguments. However, apart from the odd quotation, you do not directly copy the words in the books.

You re-write the findings of studies, and use published arguments to back up your point of view. Such is the way, I believe, that we should utilise AI as it develops and becomes an ever larger part of our world.

Here is a list of some of the platforms that offer AI-powered tools to assist with content creation. I have tried to cover what each platform does so that you can go check them out if you are interested in using AI to help build your passive income:

ChatGPT

Capabilities: Generates text, provides ideas, writes articles, assists with SEO optimization, and more.

Uses: Writing blog posts, articles, social media content, and even scripts for videos or podcasts.

Grammarly

Capabilities: Enhances writing by checking grammar, spelling, punctuation, and style. It also offers suggestions for clarity, engagement, and delivery.

Uses: Editing and proofreading content, improving readability and professionalism.

Jasper (formerly Jarvis)

Capabilities: Generates marketing copy, blog posts, product descriptions, and social media content. It can also help with SEO by suggesting keywords and content strategies.

Uses: Creating high-quality marketing content quickly and efficiently.

Copy.ai

Capabilities: Generates copy for various use cases, including blog posts, social media posts, ads, and email campaigns. It offers multiple templates and tones.

Uses: Quickly producing engaging content for marketing and communication purposes.

Canva

Capabilities: Provides AI-powered design tools for creating graphics, presentations, social media posts, and more. It includes templates, stock images, and design elements.

Uses: Designing visually appealing content for blogs, social media, presentations, and marketing materials.

SurferSEO

Capabilities: Optimizes content for search engines by analyzing top-ranking pages, suggesting keywords, and providing guidelines for content structure and length.

Uses: Enhancing SEO to improve search engine rankings and increase organic traffic.

HubSpot's Content Strategy Tool

Capabilities: Uses AI to suggest content topics, clusters, and strategies based on your existing content and industry trends.

Uses: Developing a content strategy that aligns with SEO goals and audience interests.

<u>Lumen5</u>

Capabilities: Converts blog posts and articles into engaging videos using AI. It includes templates, stock footage, and music.

Uses: Creating video content for social media, websites, and marketing campaigns.

<u>Writesonic</u>

Capabilities: Generates various forms of content, including articles, blog posts, product descriptions, and ads. It also offers AI-powered editing and rewriting tools.

Uses: Producing a wide range of written content quickly and efficiently.

<u>Wordtune</u>

Capabilities: Provides AI-powered writing suggestions to improve clarity, tone, and style. It can also help rewrite sentences and paragraphs.

Uses: Enhancing and refining written content for better readability and engagement.

<u>MarketMuse</u>

Capabilities: Uses AI to conduct content audits, suggest topics, and optimise content for SEO. It helps identify content gaps and opportunities.

Use Case: Developing data-driven content strategies and improving existing content for better SEO performance.

<u>Article Forge</u>

Capabilities: Generates unique, high-quality articles based on a few keywords. It uses deep learning models to create content that is readable and relevant.

Use Case: Quickly creating blog posts and articles with minimal input.

Each of these platforms leverages AI to streamline different aspects of content creation, from writing and editing to design and SEO optimization. By using these tools, content creators can save time, enhance the quality of their work, and improve their overall content strategy.

I have never used AI to help me write articles for my blog. I certainly will be giving it a go very soon.

Identifying your skills

You might be interested in creating content to make a passive income but aren't sure what sort of thing you can create.

Identifying your skills for content creation to generate passive income involves self-assessment, market research, and aligning your strengths with demand. Here's a step-by-step approach:

<u>Self-Assessment</u>

Start by evaluating your skills and interests:

- Professional Skills: Consider what you do in your current job or what you've done in past roles. Skills could include writing, graphic design, programming, teaching, music production, etc.

- Hobbies and Interests: Think about activities you enjoy and excel at outside of work, such as photography, crafting, gaming, or cooking.

- Education and Training: Reflect on your formal education and any additional training or certifications you have received.

- Strengths and Weaknesses: Be honest about your strong points and areas where you might need improvement.

<u>Market Research</u>

Identify what types of content are in demand:

- Trending Topics: Use tools like Google Trends, social media platforms, and industry blogs to see what's currently popular.

- Competitor Analysis:Look at what successful creators in your areas of interest are offering. Pay attention to their product types, pricing, and customer engagement.

- Audience Needs:Engage with potential audiences through forums, social media groups, and surveys to understand their needs and preferences.

<u>Matching Skills to Content Types</u>

Align your skills with suitable content formats:

- Writing: E-books, blog posts, online courses, newsletters

- Graphic Design: Printables, digital art, website templates, branding kits

- Programming:Apps, software, website themes, plugins

- Teaching: Online courses, webinars, tutorial videos

- Music: Stock music, sound effects, royalty-free tracks

- Photography/Video: Stock photos, stock videos, photo presets, video editing templates

<u>Experiment and Test</u>

Create small-scale versions of potential products to test the market:

- Minimum Viable Product (MVP): Develop a basic version of your product and release it to gather feedback.

- Pilot Projects: Run a pilot course, publish a short e-book, or release a set of printables.

- Feedback Loop: Use feedback from initial customers to refine and improve your product offerings.

Analyse Your Results

Evaluate the performance of your initial products:

- Sales Data: Track how many units you sell and at what price point.

- Customer Feedback: Collect reviews and testimonials to understand customer satisfaction.

- Engagement Metrics: Measure website traffic, social media interactions, and email open rates.

Scaling Up

Based on your analysis, focus on what works:

- Product Development: Invest more time and resources into developing full-fledged versions of your most successful products.

- Marketing Strategies: Optimise your marketing efforts based on what channels and methods drive the most sales.

- Automation: Use tools and platforms to automate processes like email marketing, social media posting, and sales tracking.

Continuous Improvement

Keep refining your products and strategies:

- Stay Updated: Keep up with industry trends and updates.

- Customer Relationships: Maintain good relationships with your customers and encourage repeat business.

- Expand Offerings: Diversify your product range based on customer needs and market trends.

By following these steps, you can effectively identify your skills, create valuable content, and build a stream of passive income.

How to make digital content

Creating and selling digital files online involves several steps, the first one being to get your work ready for sale.

Firstly you need to decide on the digital product that you want to make. We looked at this in the previous chapter.

Here is a recap of the sorts of files that people make and sell to acquire a passive income:

- E-books

- Printables (planners, art prints, templates)

- Digital art

- Music or sound effects

- Online courses or educational materials

- Software or apps

- Stock photos or videos

You then need to sit down and create your digital products.

Use appropriate tools and software to create your digital products. Here are some of the tools you can use:

<u>E-books</u>: Use Microsoft Word, Google Docs, or specialised software like Scrivener or Adobe InDesign. I use Google Docs to write my books. I like the spell checker and enjoy being able to log in and out on various devices. I upload my finished manuscripts to Kindle Create, which is software that you download onto your computer. This

produces a Kindle-ready file which you then upload onto the KDP website, which is in turn created via your Amazon account.

<u>Printables and Digital Art</u>: Use graphic design software such as Adobe Illustrator, Photoshop, or free alternatives like Canva and GIMP.

<u>Music or Sound Effects</u>: Use audio editing software like Audacity, Ableton Live, or GarageBand.

<u>Online Courses</u>: Use course creation platforms like Teachable, Thinkific, or even PowerPoint and video editing tools for recorded lectures. Canva also has some excellent editable templates.

You then need to format the files.

Ensure the files are in a suitable format for distribution:

- E-books: PDF, ePub, MOBI

- Printables: PDF, PNG, JPEG

- Digital Art: PNG, JPEG, PSD, AI

- Music: MP3, WAV

- Courses: MP4 for videos, PDF for handouts

Some creators protect their work from being copied. You may decide to

Add watermarks, for example. With self-publishing, you can anchor digital rights management (DRM), or other protective measures to prevent unauthorised distribution. When uploading books to Amazon, you will be asked if you wish to utilise DRM. It isn't as complicated as it may sound.

You then need to choose a platform to sell your digital products:

E-commerce Platforms: Shopify, WooCommerce (for WordPress).

Marketplaces: Etsy, Gumroad, Creative Market, Amazon (for e-books).

When you are ready to list your products, it is important to create compelling product listings:

<u>Title</u>: Clear and descriptive

<u>Description</u>: Detailed, highlighting the benefits and features

<u>Images</u>: High-quality images or screenshots. Do not underestimate the importance of professional-looking product photographs. I use an app called Photoroom to help with this. Regarding book covers, you can use Amazon's own cover creator, or again look to Canva for some help

<u>Price</u>: Competitive and reflective of the product's value

If you aren't using a marketplace such as eBay or Etsy, you will need to set up your own payment processing system.

Use secure payment processors such as PayPal, Stripe, or the payment systems provided by your chosen e-commerce platform.

To enhance sales to the best of your ability, it is essential to market your products.

The following will help with marketing:

Social Media: Use platforms like Instagram, Facebook, Pinterest, and Twitter

Content Marketing: Blog posts, tutorials, or videos related to your product

Email Marketing: Build an email list and send newsletters

SEO: Optimise your product listings for search engines - use keywords in your listings that buyers will type in when looking for your product.

Be prepared to assist customers with any issues or questions regarding the product or the download process. As I stated earlier, there are often emails when people don't understand how to download, or when the download process doesn't work as it should (this will happen).

As you build your portfolio of sellable digital products, make sure to constantly monitor your sales and gather feedback. This will help you to improve your products and marketing strategies.

By following these steps, you can successfully create and sell digital files online.

Finding your place

A friend of mine asked me for help in creating a passive income of her own.

I suggested a few ideas about content that I thought she might be able to create.

To every suggestion, she replied that it had already been done. She also said (in response to my proposal of helping people to understand how massage works - because she is a qualified massage therapist) that she isn't knowledgeable enough.

The thing is, whatever your knowledge of a subject, there are people who know next to nothing about it. For example, my friend could have written a course or book that introduces people to the benefits of massage, with a look at the key points to get started.

That is the sort of book I would be interested in reading. Not everyone is looking for a long, expert-level text.

Also, yes the market in some areas is oversaturated. However, one of the millionaires on the TV programme Dragons' Den once said the following: If you don't know what to do, do something that someone else is doing, but do it better.

If your content is of a high standard, there is no reason that it won't sell. We will later look at the importance of consistency. Keep going and do not give up. You will find your customers, and if your work is good, they will come back to you.

Goodness, I sell photographs on Adobe Stock. I am not a trained photographer. What sells? Not only my skin cancer images but also photos of my knitting. Not many photographers knit. I am able to provide unique, high-quality pictures of my knitted fabric fabrics and various tools and notions. I have seen my images appear on several crafting blogs, where the author needed an image to demonstrate their article. Knitting is one of my niche areas. I know a lot about it and produce a considerable amount of content based on this beloved hobby.

There is always a space for your offerings in the world of digital products. Anything that you know about, are good at or have a passion for is worth a try. If it isn't working, then change direction until you find your own successful niche.

Don't be put off by the overwhelming amount of digital content available for sale out there. Be assured that there is space for you, dear reader.

Print on Demand

Print on demand is another possibility for making a passive income. I have not personally tried this. It is potentially an oversaturated market, however I think that with a niche topic there is still money to be made.

What is print on demand?

If you ever see a mug, t-shirt, shopping bag or similar which has been printed with a slogan or image, this may well be a print on demand product.

People create the design and send it off to a print-on-demand company. The products are then integrated with a platform such as eBay, Etsy, or Shopify, and when a customer places an order the printing company will make it and send it off in the post.

It is reasonably easy to create designs. You just need imagination. You could for example specialise in cat items. Design a t-shirt with say, I would rather be a cat written on it. People looking for a gift for a cat lover may well think oh crikey that's perfect, and purchase it.

You will have already set a price based on the cost given by the printing company, and you keep whatever is over that price, minus any selling fees.

To make passive income through print on demand (POD), choosing a reliable and user-friendly company is crucial. Here are some of the best POD companies known for their quality, range of products, and ease of use:

1. <u>Printful</u>

- Pros: Extensive product catalogue, high-quality printing, integrations with major e-commerce platforms (Shopify, WooCommerce, Etsy).

- Cons: Higher base prices, shipping can be slow for international orders.

2. <u>Printify</u>

-Pros: Wide range of products, multiple print provider options, competitive pricing, integrates with major e-commerce platforms.

- Cons: Quality can vary between print providers, customer service can be inconsistent.

3. <u>Teespring (now Spring)</u>

- Pros: No upfront costs, easy to use, strong community and marketing tools, integrates with YouTube and other social media platforms.

- Cons: Limited customization options compared to other POD services, higher base prices.

4. <u>Redbubble</u>

- Pros: Large marketplace, wide variety of products, easy to use, good for artists and designers to get exposure.

- Cons: Lower profit margins, less control over branding and customer experience.

5. <u>Society6</u>

- Pros: Focus on art and design, good for artists looking to sell unique products, easy to use.

- Cons: Lower profit margins, less control over customer data.

6. Zazzle

- Pros: Huge range of customizable products, good for niche products, integrates with e-commerce platforms.

- Cons: More complex interface, lower profit margins.

7. Gooten

- Pros: Wide range of products, flexible pricing, good for scaling businesses, integrates with major e-commerce platforms.

- Cons: Quality can vary between print providers, customer service can be slow.

8. TeePublic

- Pros: Easy to use, good for selling t-shirts and apparel, large marketplace, decent profit margins.

- Cons: Limited product range compared to others, less control over branding.

9. Merch by Amazon

- Pros: Access to Amazon's massive customer base, no upfront costs, good for t-shirts and apparel.

- Cons: Competitive, limited product range, application process can be lengthy.

10. CafePress

- Pros: Wide variety of products, easy to use, good for novelty and custom gifts.

- Cons: Higher base prices, lower profit margins.

When choosing a print-on-demand company, consider factors like product range, pricing, profit margins, ease of use, integration with e-commerce platforms, and shipping options. It's often a good idea to test a few different companies to see which best meets your needs and provides the best quality for your customers.

Drop Shipping

Another possibility for making a passive income is the drop shipping business model.

How does drop shipping work?

You list for sale items that are sold by a different company, and they will package and ship the items ordered.

I have never fancied trying this. The reason is that I would worry too much about the item not being shipped on time, or being lost in the post, and so on. I guess I like to have more control than drop shipping seems to offer.

Bear in mind, this is just my opinion and many people make an excellent passive income from drop shipping. Some claim to be self made millionaires via this passive income generation method.

How to get started with drop shipping

Getting started with dropshipping can be an exciting venture, and there are many resources available to help you learn about it. Here are some of the best places to find information about dropshipping.

Online Courses and Tutorials

1. Udemy: Offers a variety of courses on dropshipping, covering everything from basics to advanced strategies.

2. Coursera: Provides courses related to e-commerce and dropshipping, often in partnership with universities.

3. Shopify Academy: Free courses and tutorials specifically tailored for dropshipping and using Shopify as a platform.

Blogs and Websites

1. Shopify Blog: Articles on dropshipping, e-commerce trends, and tips for running a successful online store.

2. Oberlo Blog: Comprehensive guides and articles specifically about dropshipping, as Oberlo is a popular dropshipping app for Shopify.

3. BigCommerce Blog: Insights into e-commerce and dropshipping strategies.

YouTube Channels

1. Wholesale Ted: Offers a lot of free content about dropshipping, including tutorials, tips, and strategies.

2. Shopify: The official Shopify YouTube channel has tutorials, success stories, and webinars related to drop shipping.

3. Oberlo: Their YouTube channel provides a wealth of information on getting started with dropshipping and optimising your store.

Forums and Communities

1. Reddit:

- r/dropshipping: A community where you can ask questions, share experiences, and learn from others.

- r/Entrepreneur: While broader than dropshipping, this subreddit has valuable insights and discussions on running a business.

2. Warrior Forum: A large community where you can find discussions about dropshipping and e-commerce.

Books

1. "Dropshipping E-Commerce Business Model 2021" by David Scott: A comprehensive guide on the basics and advanced strategies of dropshipping.

2. The Ultimate Guide to Dropshipping" by Andrew Youderian: Provides insights into running a successful dropshipping business.

Tools and Apps

1\. Oberlo: A dropshipping app that integrates with Shopify, offering resources and guides for new users.

2. Spocket: Another dropshipping app that provides resources and support for entrepreneurs.

3. AliDropship: A WordPress plugin for dropshipping that comes with a wealth of resources and support.

Webinars and Podcasts

1. Shopify Masters Podcast: Features interviews with successful e-commerce entrepreneurs, many of whom use drop shipping.

2. Oberlo's Start Yours Podcast: Focuses on stories and strategies from dropshipping entrepreneurs.

Social Media Groups

1. Facebook Groups:

- Shopify Entrepreneurs: A group where you can learn about dropshipping and get support from fellow entrepreneurs.

- Dropshipping Titans: Focuses on dropshipping strategies and support.

Engaging with these resources will help you build a strong foundation in dropshipping and stay updated on the latest trends and best practices in the industry.

Affiliate Marketing

I have briefly touched upon the topic of affiliate marketing in these pages.

Affiliate marketing is a popular way to earn money by promoting other people's products or services and earning a commission for each sale or action completed through your referral link.

I use affiliate marketing within my knitting blog - this was touched upon earlier. I thought I would explain more about this topic as there are many ways to gain a passive income by selling other companies' products in exchange for commission.

Here's a quick guide to making money from affiliate marketing:

<u>Choose a Niche</u>

- Identify Your Interests: Choose a niche that you are passionate about and knowledgeable in. This will make it easier to create content and engage with your audience.

- Market Demand: Ensure there is a demand for products or services in your chosen niche. Use tools like Google Trends, Keyword Planner, or Ahrefs to gauge interest and competition.

<u>Find Affiliate Programs</u>

- Affiliate Networks: Join affiliate networks like Amazon Associates, ShareASale, CJ Affiliate, Awin, or Rakuten. These platforms offer a variety of products and services to promote.

- Direct Affiliate Programs: Many companies have their own affiliate programs. Look for ones in your niche by searching "[product name] affiliate program."

- High Commission Offers: Evaluate commission structures and choose programs that offer competitive payouts.

Build a Platform

- Website or Blog: Create a website or blog focused on your niche. Use WordPress or other website builders to set it up.

- Content Creation: Regularly produce high-quality content that provides value to your audience. This can include blog posts, reviews, tutorials, and comparison articles.

Promote Affiliate Products

- Product Reviews: Write detailed reviews of products or services you are promoting. Highlight benefits, features, and any potential drawbacks.

- Tutorials and How-To Guides: Create content that shows how to use the product or service. Include your affiliate links within the content.

- Comparison Articles: Compare different products or services in the same category. This helps your audience make informed decisions and increases your chances of earning a commission.

- Email Marketing: Build an email list and send newsletters with valuable content and affiliate product recommendations.

Drive Traffic

- SEO: Continue optimising your content for search engines to attract more organic traffic. SEO is a field to become acquainted with once you have an online presence. It means search engine optimization and in brief, it is about using keywords that people will type in a search engine. The more you optimise your content, the more likely you will show up high in search results.

- Social Media: Promote your content on social media platforms like Facebook, Instagram, Twitter, Pinterest, and LinkedIn.

- Paid Advertising: Use Google Ads, Facebook Ads, or other paid advertising methods to drive targeted traffic to your content.

- Guest Posting: Write guest posts for other blogs or websites in your niche to build backlinks and attract new visitors.

Track Performance and Optimise

- Analytics: Use tools like Google Analytics and affiliate network dashboards to track the performance of your affiliate links.

- A/B Testing: Experiment with different types of content, link placements, and promotional strategies to see what works best.

- Optimise Content: Continuously update and optimise your content based on performance data to improve conversion rates.

Scale Your Efforts

- Expand Your Content: Create more content around your niche, including videos, podcasts, and infographics.

- Diversify Affiliate Programs: Join additional affiliate programs to offer a wider range of products and services.

- Build a Team: As your affiliate marketing business grows, consider hiring writers, SEO specialists, and social media managers to scale your efforts.

Key Tips for Success

- Be Honest: Only promote products or services that you genuinely believe in and have personally tested or researched.

- Disclose Affiliate Links: Be transparent with your audience by disclosing your affiliate relationships. This builds trust and complies with legal requirements.

- Provide Value: Focus on providing value to your audience rather than just selling products. This will build a loyal following and increase your chances of earning commissions.

By following these steps and staying committed to providing valuable content, you can build a successful affiliate marketing business and generate a steady stream of passive income.

Social Media

Now, I don't think that social media comes under the umbrella of passive income as such. However, it deserves a place in this book as there are numerous influencers out there who have managed to make a very high income over time.

I follow a married couple on Facebook who are always talking about the high income they receive just by posting photos on this platform. I believe what they say to be true because they have switched from cooking cheap meal ideas to reviewing expensive hotels and discussing their new white 'Turkey teeth'.

Fair play to this couple, they are to be greatly admired. They have spent several years building up their audience, filming and editing videos, posting photos, replying to comments, and all of the other things necessary to be successful on social media.

They recently made a post about how hard they work, and it is clear to see just from the sheer amount of content posted that what they do is far from passive. They get up very early each day, and answer emails (they seem to be making a very good income from the TikTok shop, something I will admit to knowing nothing about - worth looking into for sure).

The pair then film, edit, post, engage with followers, and do all of the other general administration involved with running a business. For making a passive income is a business just like any other.

Because of the ongoing hard work needed to make it big in social media, be it Facebook or Instagram, etc, I do not think it can be classed as a passive income. However, earlier work may still get clicks, and so over time there will be an element of passivity.

You can of course use social media for methods of earning a passive income such as affiliate marketing. This usually involves making a post about say, an air fryer that is for sale on Amazon. You could demonstrate the air fryer and post a link telling people where to buy it (your Amazon affiliate link). You would then need to pay Facebook to advertise this post so that it gets a good reach. Then it is a matter of waiting to see if anyone buys the air fryer after clicking your link.

Again though, is this passive? You would need to keep on making the videos so that they are current.

I think that making a success in social media is more dynamic and active than many other methods of content creation discussed in this book.

Social media is a fantastic tool for getting attention paid to your passive content, however. You could for example start an Instagram page highlighting your cooking, with links to your blog, youtube chanel, or book, whatever it is that you have created with an aim of earning a passive income from.

Passive income beyond content creation

Each and every one of my streams of passive income comes from content creation. Here is a summary of all of them, as written about in the previous chapters:

- Selling digital files on Etsy

- Self-publishing on Amazon And Draft2Digital

- Stock photography

- Blogging

None of the above are essentially 'passive'. They have all been extremely time-consuming, indeed it is a full-time job and I have built up the income over several years.

What you get out is what you put in, and you never get anything in exchange for nothing.

Now, if you have some cash to invest, you may not have to put in as many hours of labour to achieve a great passive income.

Investing cash to generate passive income can be a smart way to grow your wealth over time. Here are several ideas to consider:

1. Dividend Stocks

- Description: Invest in stocks that pay regular dividends.

- Pros: Potential for capital appreciation and regular income.

- Cons: Dividend payments can fluctuate, and stock prices can be volatile.

2. Real Estate

- <u>Rental Properties</u>: Purchase residential or commercial properties to rent out.

- Pros* Regular rental income, property value appreciation.

- Cons: Requires management or hiring a property manager, initial capital needed.

- <u>Real Estate Investment Trusts (REITs)</u>: Invest in publicly traded REITs.

- Pros: Dividends from real estate investments without direct management.

- Cons: Market risk similar to stocks, potential dividend cuts.

3. Bonds

- <u>Government Bonds</u>: Invest in government-issued bonds.

- Pros: Stable and predictable returns, low risk.

- Cons: Lower returns compared to other investments.

- <u>Corporate Bonds:</u> Invest in bonds issued by companies.

- Pros: Higher returns than government bonds.

- Cons: Higher risk, especially with lower-rated bonds.

4. Peer-to-Peer Lending

- Description: Lend money to individuals or small businesses through P2P platforms.

- Pros: High potential returns.

- Cons: Risk of default, less liquidity.

5. Index Funds and ETFs

- Description: Invest in a diversified portfolio of stocks or bonds.

- Pros: Low fees, broad market exposure, and typically lower risk than individual stocks.

- Cons: Market risk, returns can vary with market performance.

6. High-Yield Savings Accounts and CDs

- <u>High-Yield Savings Accounts</u>: Savings accounts with higher interest rates.

- Pros: Low risk, FDIC insured.

- Cons: Lower returns compared to other investments.

- <u>Certificates of Deposit (CDs)</u>: Fixed-term savings with higher interest rates.

- Pros: Guaranteed returns, FDIC insured.

- Cons: Less liquidity, penalties for early withdrawal.

7. Mutual Funds

- Description: Pooled funds managed by professional managers.

- Pros: Diversification, professionally managed.

- Cons: Management fees, potential market risk.

8. Royalties

- <u>Intellectual Property</u>: Invest in or create intellectual property that generates royalties (e.g., books, music, patents).

- Pros: Ongoing income from previous work.

- Cons: Initial effort and investment required.

9. <u>Annuities</u>

- Description: Insurance products that provide regular payments in exchange for an initial lump sum.

- Pros: Guaranteed income, tax benefits.

- Cons: Fees, less liquidity, lower returns compared to other investments.

10. Business Investments

- Description: Invest in a business either as a silent partner or through equity crowdfunding.

- Pros: Potential for high returns, involvement in growing companies.

- Cons: High risk, potential for loss if the business fails.

11. Cryptocurrency Staking and Yield Farming

- <u>Staking</u>: Earn rewards by holding and supporting the network of a cryptocurrency.

- Pros: High potential returns, passive income.

- Cons: High risk, volatility, potential technical challenges.

- <u>Yield Farming</u>: Earn interest or rewards by lending or providing liquidity to DeFi platforms.

- Pros: High potential returns.

- Cons* High risk, potential for loss due to platform hacks or volatility.

12. Automated Investment Services (Robo-Advisors)

- Description: Invest through platforms that use algorithms to manage your portfolio.

- Pros: Low fees, diversified portfolio, hands-off approach.

- Cons: Limited customization, market risk.

When considering any investment for passive income, it's important to assess your risk tolerance, time horizon, and financial goals. Diversifying your investments can also help mitigate risks and enhance the stability of your passive income streams.

A friend of mine has managed to save up over £100,000 purely from going to work since a young age. She has chosen to place all of her capital into high-yield savings accounts. She receives around £250 interest per month and is perfectly happy with this passive income.

Another friend of mine has savings in the amount of £15,000. He has spent the whole lot on cryptocurrency, and indeed on one particular coin. This coin is called Kaspa and my friend is confident that he will have made at least half a million pounds in 6-7 years time.

I see these two methods of passive income via cash investment as polar opposites. One is safe, regulated, and predictable. The crypto investment is a high risk, with no safety blanket whatsoever. My friend could lose all of his cash. But with his (what is in my opinion) gamble, he may indeed end up a very wealthy man. Time will tell.

I personally wouldn't dare invest in cryptocurrency. However, many people claim to have become millionaires by doing exactly that.

Determining the exact number of people who have become millionaires from cryptocurrency is challenging due to the private nature of individual wealth and the volatility of the market. However, several sources and studies provide some insights:

Estimates and Studies

1. Forbes and Media Reports:

- In 2021, Forbes identified several dozen individuals who had amassed significant wealth from cryptocurrency investments, including notable figures like the Winklevoss twins, Vitalik Buterin (co-founder of Ethereum), and others. These lists often highlight the most prominent and wealthiest individuals but don't capture the broader population of crypto millionaires.

2. Crypto Exchanges and Companies:

- Executives and early employees of major cryptocurrency companies and exchanges (e.g., Coinbase, Binance) have likely become millionaires due to the significant valuation of these companies.

3. Blockchain Data Analysis:

- Blockchain analytics firms like Chainalysis and Glassnode provide insights into the distribution of wealth on the blockchain. They often report on the number of addresses holding substantial amounts of cryptocurrency. However, since individuals can own multiple addresses, these numbers don't directly translate to the number of millionaires.

4. General Estimates:

- Various articles and estimates from financial news outlets have suggested that there are thousands, potentially tens of thousands, of crypto millionaires. For example, a 2021 report by cryptocurrency exchange Crypto.com estimated that there were over 100 million cryptocurrency users worldwide, and a fraction of these users have become millionaires due to the significant price appreciation of assets like Bitcoin and Ethereum.

Factors Influencing the Number of Crypto Millionaires

1. Early Adoption:

- Many early adopters of Bitcoin and other cryptocurrencies, who invested when prices were very low, have seen substantial gains, often reaching millionaire status.

2. Market Volatility:

- The highly volatile nature of cryptocurrency markets means that the number of millionaires can fluctuate significantly with market cycles. Bull markets can create new millionaires, while bear markets can erode wealth.

3. Investment in ICOs and Altcoins:

- Some investors who participated in initial coin offerings (ICOs) or invested in altcoins that experienced significant price increases have also become millionaires.

4. Geographical Distribution:

- Cryptocurrency adoption and wealth distribution can vary significantly by region, with some areas having a higher concentration of crypto millionaires.

While precise numbers are elusive, it is clear that cryptocurrency has created a significant number of millionaires, particularly among early adopters and savvy investors who navigated the market's ups and downs.

If you are looking to invest your capital to make a passive income, either by traditional (safer) methods or by investment into cryptocurrency, here are some considerations to make regarding safety and reliability:

- <u>Diversification</u>: Spread investments across different asset classes to reduce risk.

- <u>Research</u>: Understand the risks and benefits of each investment option.

- <u>Time Horizon</u>: Align investments with your financial goals and time frame.

- <u>Professional Advice</u>: Consider consulting a financial advisor to tailor a strategy to your needs.

Each of these options offers a balance of safety and reliability, making them suitable for investors seeking steady passive income with minimal risk.

Seeking financial advice when investing money to generate passive income is a wise decision. Here are several reasons why:

<u>1. Personalized Investment Strategy</u>

- Tailored Advice: A financial advisor can help create a personalised investment strategy based on your individual financial situation, goals, risk tolerance, and time horizon.

- Comprehensive Planning: Advisors consider all aspects of your financial life, including taxes, retirement planning, estate planning, and more.

2. Risk Management

- Risk Assessment: Financial advisors can assess your risk tolerance and recommend investments that align with your comfort level.

- Diversification: Advisors can help you diversify your portfolio to mitigate risk and reduce the impact of market volatility.

3. Expert Knowledge

- Market Insights: Advisors have access to the latest market research and insights, which can inform better investment decisions.

- Complex Products: They can explain complex financial products and strategies that you might not be familiar with, such as annuities, REITs, or bond funds.

4. Long-Term Focus

- Discipline: Advisors can help you stay focused on your long-term goals, avoiding impulsive decisions driven by short-term market fluctuations.

- Regular Reviews: They provide ongoing portfolio reviews and adjustments to ensure your investments remain aligned with your objectives.

5. Tax Efficiency

- Tax Strategies: Advisors can suggest tax-efficient investment strategies, helping you maximize your after-tax returns.

- Tax Planning: They can help with tax planning, such as the timing of asset sales and choosing tax-advantaged accounts.

6. Emotional Support

- Market Volatility: During periods of market volatility, an advisor can provide reassurance and prevent you from making emotionally driven decisions that could harm your long-term financial health.

7. Access to Exclusive Opportunities

- Institutional Products: Financial advisors often have access to investment products and opportunities not available to individual investors.

- Network: They might connect you with other professionals, such as tax advisors or estate planners, to provide comprehensive financial planning.

8. Regulatory and Compliance Assurance

- Compliance: Advisors ensure that your investments comply with regulatory requirements.

- Fiduciary Duty: Many advisors are fiduciaries, meaning they are legally required to act in your best interest.

When to Seek Financial Advice

- Large Sum of Money: If you're investing a significant amount of money, professional advice can help manage it effectively.

- Complex Financial Situation: If you have a complex financial situation with multiple goals, assets, and liabilities.

- Lack of Expertise: If you lack the knowledge or experience to confidently manage your investments.

- Major Life Changes: During major life events like retirement, inheritance, or selling a business.

I advise you to seek financial advice in all cases of investing money.

FINDING THE RIGHT FINANCIAL Advisor

- Credentials: Look for certified professionals such as CFP (Certified Financial Planner) or CFA (Chartered Financial Analyst).

- Reputation: Check reviews, ask for referrals, and ensure they have a good track record.

- Fee Structure: Understand how they charge for their services (e.g., flat fee, hourly rate, percentage of assets under management).

In conclusion, while it's possible to manage your investments independently, a financial advisor can provide valuable expertise, peace of mind, and potentially better outcomes for your passive income goals.

Other than seeking financial advice, where is a good place for beginners to begin with buying stocks, shares and cryptocurrencies?

If you are a beginner looking to invest in cryptocurrencies or stocks and shares, there are several user-friendly online platforms that offer these services. Here are some popular ones:

Platforms for Buying Cryptocurrencies:

1. Coinbase

- Features: Easy-to-use interface, educational resources, secure storage options, supports a wide range of cryptocurrencies.

- Ideal For: Beginners looking to buy, sell, and store cryptocurrencies.

<u>2. Binance</u>

- Features: Wide variety of cryptocurrencies, advanced trading features, lower fees, and educational resources.

- Ideal For: Beginners and intermediate users who want access to a wide range of crypto assets and trading options.

<u>3. Kraken</u>

- Features: User-friendly interface, comprehensive security measures, supports a wide range of cryptocurrencies, and staking options.

- Ideal For: Beginners looking for a secure platform with a good range of supported cryptocurrencies.

<u>4. Gemini</u>

- Features: Simple interface, strong security features, insured crypto storage, educational resources.

- Ideal For: Beginners who prioritize security and ease of use.

Platforms for Buying Stocks and Shares:

<u>1. Robinhood</u>

- Features: Commission-free trades, user-friendly mobile app, fractional shares, access to cryptocurrencies.

- Ideal For: Beginners who want a simple way to start investing in stocks and cryptocurrencies with no fees.

<u>2. E*TRADE</u>

- Features: Extensive research tools, educational resources, commission-free trades for stocks and ETFs, and retirement accounts.

- Ideal For: Beginners who want robust research tools and a wide range of investment options.

3. Fidelity

- Features: No commissions for online stock and ETF trades, extensive research and educational tools, and excellent customer service.

- Ideal For: Beginners looking for comprehensive support and a trusted name in investment.

4. Charles Schwab

- Features: Commission-free stock and ETF trades, extensive research tools, fractional shares, and educational resources.

- Ideal For: Beginners who want a full-service brokerage with a wide range of investment options.

5. Webull

- Features: Commission-free trades, advanced charting tools, access to cryptocurrencies, fractional shares.

- Ideal For: Beginners and intermediate investors who want more advanced tools and features.

Platforms for Both Cryptocurrencies and Stocks:

1. eToro

- Features: Supports both crypto and stock trading, social trading features, educational resources, and user-friendly interface.

- Ideal For: Beginners who want to diversify their investments and follow other traders' strategies.

2. SoFi Invest

- Features: No-fee stock and ETF trading, crypto trading, automated investing options, educational resources.

- Ideal For: Beginners looking for a holistic approach to investing with a range of options from one platform.

<u>3. Cash App</u>

- Features: Simple interface, allows purchase of Bitcoin and stocks, instant deposits, easy-to-use.

- Ideal For: Beginners looking for an ultra-simplified way to invest in both stocks and Bitcoin.

Tips for Beginners:

- Start Small: Begin with small investments to get familiar with the platforms and how the market works.

- Education: Utilize the educational resources provided by these platforms to build your understanding of investing.

- Diversification: Spread your investments across different assets to minimize risk.

- Research: Regularly research and stay informed about the investments you make.

- Security: Use platforms with strong security measures to protect your investments.

By choosing the right platform based on your needs and investing style, you can begin your journey into investing with confidence and ease.

Can AI help with investing money in the hope of making a passive income?

AI CAN HELP YOU INVEST your money to make a passive income through various means. Here are some ways AI can assist with investments:

1. <u>Robo-Advisors:</u>

- Automated Investment Management: Robo-advisors use AI to manage your investment portfolio automatically. They can handle tasks like asset allocation, rebalancing, and tax-loss harvesting based on your risk tolerance and investment goals.

- Personalised Recommendations: AI algorithms can provide tailored investment strategies based on your financial situation, preferences, and long-term goals.

2. <u>Algorithmic Trading:</u>

- Automated Trading Systems: AI-powered trading systems can execute trades on your behalf based on predefined criteria and market conditions. These systems can react quickly to market changes and potentially capitalise on short-term opportunities.

- Market Analysis: AI can analyse vast amounts of market data, news, and trends to identify potential investment opportunities and generate trading signals.

3. <u>Predictive Analytics:</u>

- Market Prediction*: AI models can predict market trends and price movements using historical data, sentiment analysis, and other factors. While not foolproof, these predictions can help inform your investment decisions.

- Risk Assessment: AI can evaluate the risk associated with different investments, helping you make more informed choices that align with your risk tolerance.

4. <u>Portfolio Optimization:</u>

- Diversification Strategies: AI can help diversify your portfolio by identifying a mix of assets that can minimise risk while maximising returns.

- Performance Monitoring: AI can continuously monitor your portfolio's performance and suggest adjustments to optimise returns and manage risk.

5. <u>Sentiment Analysis:</u>

- Social Media and News Analysis: AI can analyse sentiment from social media, news articles, and other online sources to gauge public opinion and market sentiment about particular stocks or sectors.

- Impact Assessment: AI can assess how news events or changes in public sentiment might impact your investments and suggest appropriate actions.

6. <u>Financial Planning:</u>

- Goal Setting: AI can help you set realistic financial goals and create a comprehensive plan to achieve them.

- Savings and Budgeting: AI tools can analyse your spending habits and provide recommendations for saving more effectively and budgeting better to allocate funds for investments.

7. <u>Custom Investment Products:</u>

- Thematic Investing: AI can help you invest in themes or sectors you are passionate about, such as green energy or technology, by identifying relevant investment opportunities.

- Custom ETFs and Mutual Funds: Some platforms use AI to create customised ETFs and mutual funds tailored to your preferences and risk profile.

8. <u>Real Estate Investment:</u>

- Property Valuation: AI can analyse real estate market data to provide accurate property valuations and identify potential investment properties.

- Rental Income Optimization: AI can help optimise rental income by analysing market trends and suggesting competitive rental rates.

9. <u>Peer-to-Peer Lending:</u>

- Risk Assessment: AI can assess the creditworthiness of borrowers in peer-to-peer lending platforms, helping you choose less risky investment opportunities.

- Portfolio Management: AI can help diversify your lending portfolio to spread risk and improve returns.

By leveraging AI in these ways, you can potentially make more informed investment decisions, optimise your portfolio, and generate passive earnings with a reduced level of active management.

However, it is important to remember that all investments carry risk, and it's essential to complement AI-driven insights with your own research and advice from financial professionals.

Manifestation

I wholeheartedly believe in the power of manifestation.

Manifestation is the practice of bringing thoughts, desires, or goals into reality through focused intention and belief. The concept is rooted in the idea that by thinking positively and believing in the possibility of achieving a specific outcome, you can attract that outcome into your life.

Key elements of manifestation include:

1. Clarity: Clearly define what you want to achieve. This involves setting specific, measurable goals and having a detailed vision of the desired outcome.

2. Visualisation: Imagining the desired outcome as if it has already happened. This process helps to reinforce belief and align your mindset with your goals.

3. Affirmations: Repeating positive statements about your goals and your ability to achieve them. This practice helps to build confidence and reinforce positive thinking.

4. Belief: Truly believing that what you desire is possible and that you are capable of achieving it. This belief is crucial as it influences your actions and attitude.

5. Action: Taking concrete steps toward your goals. While thought and belief are important, taking actionable steps is essential for turning desires into reality.

6. Gratitude: Practising gratitude for what you already have and for the progress you make. This helps to maintain a positive mindset and attract more positive experiences.

I have included manifestation in this book because I believe the use of this practice is essential if you truly desire to achieve a level of wealth via the creation of a passive income.

You see, to achieve anything worthwhile in life, you need to have both a plan and a goal. And you can't plan anything without a goal.

Why do you want to earn a passive income? How much would you like to make? What is your time limit to reach your goal?

When you know the answer to the latter two questions, write this down with pen and paper.

For example:

I will make a passive income of £1000 per month.

The £1000 a month payment will start appearing in my bank account by the end of next year.

Maybe you want to make more money, in a shorter time. Whatever it is you dream of or need, write it down. Read out loud what you have written on your sheet paper every morning upon waking and every night before you retire to bed.

Now, what are you going to do/give to make this goal a reality?

To achieve your dreams, you have to give something. There is a trade. If you neither give nor do anything, whatever it is you wish to manifest isn't going to happen.

By having a plan, and putting it into action, you reaffirm in your mind that you CAN achieve your goal within the stated time frame. Your journey has begun, you are about to change your life. The Universe will respond to your newfound energy and positivity by delivering that which you desire.

This is the essence of manifestation. Aim, plan, and see the dream become a reality.

It can sometimes be the case that your initial plan to achieve your goal doesn't seem to be working. Do not worry, the Universe will show you the way. You may have a thought, a feeling, or a sign. Perhaps a brilliant-sounding idea will pop into your head when you are thinking about something completely different.

Listen to all of these signs and follow your gut instincts, always. And don't ever give up. If you want that £1000 per month (or that 1 million per month, why not?) and you keep at it, and keep believing that you shall have it with all of your heart and mind, you shall have it.

Sow the seeds of your garden well, water it regularly and consistently, and in time you will be basking in the life-enhancing beauty of its maturity.

Consistency is key

I mentioned earlier in the book that I consider myself to be a jack of all trades and master of none.

I have several streams of passive income and this can be seen as positive, impressive even.

The reason my portfolio is so varied is that I am curious. I have dipped in and out of several projects to see how each area of interest worked and how easy it was or not to make a living.

The thing is, when you run a business, one of the most important factors that determines success or failure is consistency.

Let us use my blog to demonstrate my current point. I started a blog and used to publish 1-2 articles per week. I was publishing free knitting patterns and lists of useful tips, for example where to find the best sock knitting patterns.

Follower numbers began to grow and my revenue from ads began to climb. Then I moved on to the next shiny object and currently I only publish one article every four to six weeks.

If you lose interest in your endeavour, so will your customers/readers/supporters.

Consistency brings about what is known as a cumulative effect. Suddenly, everything comes together and your business endeavour will bloom.

I think that juggling too many balls in the air can be bad for your mental health. Some days I have so many things that I want to do that all I actually manage is a day sitting on the sofa doing absolutely nothing.

I often really wish I could just do one thing. But when I try to cut back, I feel guilty and worry that I have made a mistake by not doing the other thing.

I bet even reading about this dilemma of mine is exhausting, isn't it?

Let us have a quick look at the cumulative effect in business, to show us the importance of being consistent

The cumulative effect in business, when you are consistent, refers to the compounding benefits that result from sustained and regular efforts over time. This concept is similar to compound interest in finance, where small, regular contributions grow exponentially. Here are several key aspects of the cumulative effect in business due to consistency:

1. Brand Recognition and Trust

- Consistency in Branding: Regular use of logos, colour schemes, and messaging across all platforms builds brand recognition.

- Customer Trust: Delivering consistent quality in products and services builds customer trust and loyalty.

2. Customer Relationships and Retention

- Reliable Customer Service: Consistent, high-quality customer service fosters long-term relationships and encourages repeat business.

- Customer Experience: Providing a consistently positive customer experience leads to higher satisfaction and retention rates.

3. Operational Efficiency

- Process Improvement: Regularly refining and following standardised processes improves efficiency and reduces errors.

- Training and Development: Consistent training and development programs ensure employees are skilled and aligned with company goals.

4. Financial Stability and Growth

- Predictable Revenue: Consistent sales and revenue generation create financial stability, making it easier to plan and invest in growth.

- Cost Management: Consistent cost control measures lead to better financial management and profitability.

5. Market Presence and Expansion

- Marketing Efforts: Consistent marketing efforts, such as regular content updates and advertising, keep your brand visible and relevant.

- Market Penetration: Regularly introducing new products or services based on market research helps in capturing and expanding market share.

6. Employee Morale and Productivity

- Work Environment: A consistent and positive work environment boosts employee morale and productivity.

- Clear Expectations: Consistently communicated expectations and feedback help employees understand their roles and perform better.

7. Reputation Management

- Consistent Quality: Maintaining high standards consistently enhances your reputation and attracts more customers and partners.

- Crisis Management: Regularly updating and practising crisis management plans prepares your business to handle issues effectively, preserving your reputation.

8. Innovation and Adaptation

- Ongoing Improvement: Regularly seeking and implementing feedback leads to continuous improvement and innovation.

- Market Adaptation: Consistent monitoring of market trends allows your business to adapt and stay competitive.

Examples of the Cumulative Effect in Business

- Content Marketing: Regularly publishing valuable content (blogs, videos, etc.) builds an audience over time, improving SEO and generating leads.

- Customer Loyalty Programs: Consistent rewards for repeat customers enhance loyalty and increase lifetime value.

- Networking: Regularly attending industry events and engaging with peers builds a strong professional network, leading to more opportunities.

The cumulative effect of consistency in business can lead to exponential growth and long-term success. By focusing on regular, sustained efforts across various aspects of your business, you can build a strong foundation that compounds over time, resulting in significant improvements in brand recognition, customer loyalty, operational efficiency, financial stability, and overall market presence.

I guess what I am saying is, learn from my mistakes. Don't overburden yourself. I think it is better to have time and passion in one or two areas. Concentrate fully on fewer things, and become superb at delivering in your chosen specialties.

It is difficult to be consistent, and reach the cumulative benefits discussed above, if you have too much going on. Something will always suffer and you may indeed burn yourself and end up doing nothing.

That is my experience anyway.

Of course, we do not all function in the same way, and you must do whatever works best for you.

I recently wrote out a daily task timetable, and when I can't decide what to do I will look at the timetable and do whatever is written there. I have to say that this really has increased productivity.

Doing something, rather than sitting down trying to decide what to do, is certainly the most profitable track to travel down.

Find out more about making a passive income

Here are some recommendations for further reading or watching, should you wish to find out more about the topic of making a passive income.

Online Courses and Tutorials

1. Udemy: Offers a variety of courses on passive income strategies, including real estate, stock market investing, and online businesses.

2. Coursera: Provides courses from universities that cover topics related to passive income, such as investment strategies and entrepreneurship.

3. Skillshare: Offers courses on creating digital products, affiliate marketing, and other passive income streams.

Blogs and Websites

1. Smart Passive Income: Pat Flynn's blog is a comprehensive resource on various passive income strategies, including blogging, affiliate marketing, and online business.

2. Investopedia: Contains articles and guides on investing in stocks, real estate, and other passive income opportunities.

3. The Penny Hoarder: Offers articles on side hustles, investments, and other ways to generate passive income.

YouTube Channels

1. Graham Stephan: Covers real estate investing, stock market investments, and other passive income strategies.

2. Pat Flynn - Smart Passive Income: Shares tips and strategies on building online businesses and generating passive income.

3. Ali Abdaal: Discusses multiple streams of passive income, including digital products, YouTube, and investments.

Books

1. "Rich Dad Poor Dad" by Robert Kiyosaki: Offers insights into building wealth through passive income and smart investments.

2. "The 4-Hour Workweek by Timothy Ferriss: Explores how to create automated systems to generate income with minimal effort.

3. "Passive Income, Aggressive Retirement" by Rachel Richard: Provides detailed strategies for creating passive income streams.

Forums and Communities

1. Reddit:

- r/Passive_Income: A subreddit dedicated to discussing and sharing passive income ideas and strategies.

- r/Entrepreneur: While broader in scope, this subreddit has valuable discussions on passive income and business strategies.

2. BiggerPockets: A community focused on real estate investing, a common and lucrative passive income strategy.

Podcasts

1. The Smart Passive Income Podcast: Hosted by Pat Flynn, it features interviews with successful entrepreneurs who share their passive income strategies.

2. BiggerPockets Real Estate Podcast: Focuses on real estate investing as a means to generate passive income.

3. The Side Hustle School Podcast: Offers daily episodes on side hustles that can evolve into passive income streams.

Websites and Platforms for Specific Passive Income Streams

1. Real Estate:

- Roofstock: A marketplace for buying and selling rental properties.

- Fundrise: A platform for investing in real estate projects.

2. Stock Market and Dividends:

- Robinhood: A brokerage platform that makes it easy to invest in stocks and ETFs.

- Dividend.com: Provides information on dividend investing.

3. Digital Products and Online Businesses:

- Teachable: Create and sell online courses.

- Amazon Kindle Direct Publishing: Self-publish eBooks.

- Shopify: Build an e-commerce store for dropshipping or selling products.

Social Media Groups

1. Facebook Groups:

- Passive Income & Financial Independence: A group where members share tips and strategies for achieving financial independence through passive income.

- Real Estate Investing for Passive Income: Focuses on generating passive income through real estate investments.

Webinars and Seminars

1. Webinars hosted by financial advisors and investment platforms: Many financial advisors and platforms like Vanguard, Fidelity, and others offer webinars on investment strategies.

2. Online business seminars: Websites like Eventbrite often list seminars and workshops on creating online businesses and passive income streams.

By exploring these resources, you are able to gain a further understanding of various passive income strategies.

About SEO

SEO - search engine optimisation - has been mentioned a few times in this book.

In a nutshell, SEO is about enhancing the chances that people will find your content when they enter queries into a search engine such as Google.

There are entire courses and books devoted to this topic, and I am not proclaiming to be an expert in SEO.

Here is a quick explanation at how people go about optimising their online presence using the principles of SEO:

- To optimise SEO in your online content or website, focus on keyword research to identify terms your audience is searching for, and strategically incorporate these keywords into your titles, headers, and throughout your content.

- Ensure your website is technically sound with fast loading times, mobile-friendly design, and clean URLs.

- Create high-quality, relevant content that provides value to your visitors, and regularly update it to keep it fresh.

- Use internal linking to connect related pages improve site navigation, and build backlinks from reputable sites to boost your site's authority.

- Leverage meta tags, including meta descriptions and alt text for images, to improve search engine indexing and enhance user experience.

Learning about SEO (Search Engine Optimization) is crucial for improving the visibility and ranking of your website or product listings in search engine results.

Here are some recommended sources to learn about SEO:

<u>Online Courses and Tutorials</u>

1. Coursera:

- SEO Specialization by UC Davis: A comprehensive course that covers all aspects of SEO.

2. Udemy:

- SEO 2023: Complete SEO Training + SEO for WordPress Websites: Updated courses that cover SEO fundamentals and advanced techniques.

3. LinkedIn Learning:

- SEO Foundations**: Offers a solid introduction to SEO principles and practices.

<u>Blogs and Websites</u>

1. Moz Blog:

- Provides in-depth articles and resources on various SEO topics, tools, and updates.

2. Ahrefs Blog:

- Offers practical SEO advice, case studies, and detailed guides.

3. Search Engine Journal:

- Covers the latest SEO news, trends, and expert insights.

4. Backlinko:

- Brian Dean's blog, known for its comprehensive and actionable SEO guides and techniques.

YouTube Channels

1. Ahrefs:

- Offers tutorials, case studies, and industry insights.

2. Neil Patel:

- Provides SEO tips, strategies, and tutorials in an easy-to-understand format.

3. Moz:

- Features Whiteboard Friday videos that explain various SEO concepts and strategies.

Books

1. "The Art of SEO" by Eric Enge, Stephan Spencer, and Jessie Stricchiola**:

- A comprehensive guide that covers SEO strategies in detail.

2. "SEO 2023: Learn Search Engine Optimization" by Adam Clarke:

- Offers up-to-date SEO tactics and strategies.

3. "SEO for Dummies" by Peter Kent:

- A beginner-friendly book that explains SEO basics in a straightforward manner.

Forums and Communities

1. Reddit:

- r/SEO: A community for discussing SEO strategies, news, and updates.

2. SEO Chat Forums:

- A place to ask questions and share knowledge with other SEO professionals.

3. Warrior Forum:

- A large community with discussions on various digital marketing and SEO topics.

Tools and Resources

1. Google Search Central (formerly Google Webmasters):

- Official documentation and guidelines from Google on best practices for SEO.

2. SEMrush Academy:

- Free courses on SEO and digital marketing using SEMrush tools.

3. Yoast SEO Blog:

- Offers tips and insights on optimising WordPress websites with the Yoast SEO plugin.

Webinars and Podcasts

1. SEO 101 Podcast:

- A podcast that covers basic to advanced SEO topics and trends.

2. The MozPod:

- Moz's official podcast featuring interviews with SEO experts and discussions on the latest SEO news.

3. Edge of the Web Radio:

- Focuses on SEO, digital marketing, and trending topics in the industry.

By exploring these sources, you can build a strong foundation in SEO, and learn how to bring more traffic to your online undertakings.

A final word

This book has covered many different areas of passive income generation.

You will also have found numerous further sources of advice and help, should you wish to explore more.

It may be that you are overwhelmed with all of the information given, and are still wondering, "But where do I start?".

<u>I will try to break it all down for you here:</u>

The very first step is to think how much money you would like to make, and in what timescale (see Manifestation chapter).

Then identify what skills you have, and what you enjoy doing (for the all-important consistency, it has to be interesting and fit your skill set).

Are you a writer? Then consider self-publishing or blogging. If blogging, you made decide to utilise affiliate marketing and advertising placement to make an income.

Perhaps your skills lie in creating digital art, such as vectors. You can upload these to stock websites and receive a payment each time your work is licensed. You could also/alternatively sell your work on platforms such as Etsy or Creative Market. Offering your work on your own website using a tool such as Sellfy may also be an option for you.

Do you love making videos? Try out making a YouTube channel. With enough views and subscribers, you will receive a passive income via watched adverts. Facebook is another platform that pays for well-watched videos.

Would you like to speculate with your capital and invest in stocks and shares? Take a look at platforms such as Etoro - you can buy and sell here as well as learn how to maximise your earning potential.

Whatever your choice of method to create passive income streams, consistency is key. Think of the endgame. If you try it all out for a couple of weeks and then give up, success just won't happen. You have to keep going until you find something that works for you, rinse and repeat.

Tap into the wealth of information that is out there to teach you about making a passive income. Find your niche. Focus on what it is that you are trying to achieve, and put in the work to get it.

If other people can make a passive income and give up their regular jobs, so can you, if that is your aim.

Many successful passive income makers have written books and blogs, made videos and shared their story in various other ways in the internet. Learn from these people. However, be wary of 'gurus' who make fake claims about the level of their success.

I would like to thank you most sincerely for reading this book.

I hope you have found it helpful.

I would like to take this opportunity to wish you every success in your pursuit of a passive income, and indeed with everything that you wish to achieve in your life.

Remember, do not ever give up on your dreams.